NEW ETHICS PROVED IN GEOMETRICAL ORDER

Spinozist Reflexions on Evolutionary Systems

Exploring Unity Through Diversity
Volume 2

NEW ETHICS PROVED IN GEOMETRICAL ORDER

Spinozist Reflexions on Evolutionary Systems

Rainer E. Zimmermann

EMERGENT™
PUBLICATIONS

New Ethics Proved in Geometrical Order
Spinozist Reflexions on Evolutionary Systems
Written by: Rainer E. Zimmermann

Library of Congress Control Number: 2010917486

ISBN: 978-0-9842165-1-2

Copyright © 2010
Emergent Publications,
3810 N. 188th Ave, Litchfield Park, AZ 85340, USA

Printed in the United States of America

About the Book Series:
Exploring Unity through Diversity

*U*nity through Diversity is acknowledged to be the leitmotif of Ludwig von Bertalanffy's thinking. It is also the leitmotif of this series; that is, providing space for different perspectives while sharing a common goal in order to promote:

- Systems sciences, cybernetics and sciences of complexity as the most promising approaches towards global challenges humanity is facing in the new millennium;

- Transdisciplinarity and consilience throughout all scientific disciplines;

- The discussion and comparison of different schools of systems thinking;

- Attempts to unify systems thinking and to elaborate a meta-theoretical framework;

- Systems history;

- Critical reflections of the development of systems thinking and the systems movement;

- Revisiting the goals of General System Theory as set by Ludwig von Bertalanffy, Anatol Rapoport, Kenneth Boulding and others;

- Social-scientific, that is, socio-economic, political, cultural and historical applications of systems thinking, including ecological and science-and-technology studies applications;

- Systems philosophy, and;

- Monographs or volumes of collected contributions in systems

About This Volume

"Bertalanffy meets Spinoza", says Zimmermann. He makes them meet in the perspective of evolutionary systems. In reaching out for the whole, both Spinoza and Bertalanffy were aware of the tension between the formal and the informal, between strict logical-mathematical formalization and hermeneutic considerations that are not as strict. Zimmermann shows how those two approaches can complement each other and how much Spinoza can be regarded as a forerunner of modern systems thinking as well. By presenting new conceptualizations like that of the relation between systems, networks and space, he reconstructs Spinoza's ethics as the quest for adequate behavior given the knowledge at hand.

Wolfgang Hofkirchner
November, 2010

About The Author

Rainer E. Zimmermann holds both a PhD in mathematics and in philosophy. He has done his habilitation on Philosophy of Nature at the University of Kassel, Germany. He is presently Professor of Philosophy at the University of Applied Science in Munich, Germany, Senior Lecturer at the Institute of Philosophy at the University of Kassel as well as Life Member of Clare Hall, University of Cambridge, UK. He works on a unified approach to philosophy, aiming at an Ethics which is derived from Metaphysics and Philosophy of Nature including Philosophy of Science (particularly of quantum gravity theories), and also on the relationship between ontological and epistemological consequences of perceiving, linguistic modeling and designing of the world, especially in terms of spaces, networks, and (evolutionary) systems.

About the Bertalanffy Center for the Study of Systems Science (BCSSS)

Given the global challenges of today, systems science is needed more than ever. Yet system theory is not mainstream. The objective of the BCSSS is to inspire the development of systems science. The BCSSS aims at the advancement of scientific research in the field of systems thinking. In particular, it revisits General System Theory (GST) as founded by Ludwig von Bertalanffy and others in order to reassess it in the light of today's global challenges and to illuminate the course of development systems science has taken since. The BCSSS is open to cooperation with every person or organization supporting he same aim. The BCSSS owns the Ludwig von Bertalanffy archive and possesses a collection of publications of the systems movement.

Website: http://www.bertalanffy.org/

For further information please contact:

Hofkirchner Wolfgang, Prof. Dr.
BCSSS
c/o Institute for Design and Technology Assessment
Vienna University of Technology
Favoritenstr. 9-11/E187

1040 Vienna
Austria

wolfgang.hofkirchner@tuwien.ac.at

Contents

Preface

It goes without saying that today, we cannot simply take Spinoza's results and apply them to our present research problems. The context within which Spinoza once developed his theory has clearly changed by now. However, the philosopher in general is not only trying to unify the scientific world view of his/her epoch, instead he/she is also attempting a structural outline of how human beings should *think* properly, due to universal aspects which are deeply rooted in the anthropological basis of philosophy itself. Indeed, it is this framework of an inventory of discourse which represents the human activity of reflexion in the first place, and which according to a generalized concept Sartre once took from Hegel could be called *objective spirit* that we can utilize as a starting point for present research, namely in terms of a *structural guideline* for present and future problems, provided an adequate modification is taken into account in the conceptualizing procedure itself. Hence, some ideas of Spinoza's are still valid after the roughly 350 years that have elapsed since the production of most of his works. Other ideas have to be given up, especially those that relate to the close interaction between philosophy and science on the one hand and theology on the other characteristic for the 17th century. As it turns out (and this will be the main topic of this present text), most of Spinoza's general approach to conceptualizing the world can still be utilized, given a slight change in terminology. In particular, we will argue here that Spinoza's approach has many advantages as compared with approaches of his contemporaries such as Descartes and Leibniz. And we will also argue that it is the traditional main line of (primarily hermeneutic) thinking which unfolds in Spinoza's system of propositions that is far more effective in the long run as compared to more recent approaches, especially of the theory type which is called *analytical* nowadays. On the other hand, we will notice that conceptualization today does also mean to take fields such as physics and mathematics explicitly into account. This is a somewhat counterintuitive point, if judged in terms of most of the philosophy of the past 200 years at least. But after all, as it turns out, it is a point which is very much in the sense of Spinoza's original intention which led him to speak in his main work of an *ethics* which would be proved *in geometrical order* (which actually means: according to mathematical methods). In fact, Spinoza would have been happy about a mathematical machinery which is based on a strict logical structure as well as on a not so strict *hermeneutic* structure—*and* is even representable in terms of algebraic expressions of a considerable symbolic quality. This is what we try to demonstrate here for us today, given the mentioned main line of Spinoza's argument. Eventually, this may be capable of shedding a completely new light on the ancient problem of the relationship between human beings and the rest of nature. As we will see in this present text, the theory of evolutionary systems is a prime candidate for a conceptualization that might be useful in order to concretely develop this new insight. Obviously, this approach is also very much in the sense of one of the founding fathers of systems theory: Ludwig von Bertalanffy. He also started from a holistic perspective which for his time (when he actually emerged from the vicinity of the Vienna school) was not more equally natural than it was at the time of Spinoza. Essentially, he thought that the laws of biological systems such as those governing growth and adaptation of living beings might well be applicable to the human psyche, to social institutions, and to the global ecosphere altogether. He thought that the natural laws of organization would govern systems on all levels of existence. And the search for these laws he called *General Systems Theory*, although it might have been visualized as a method rather than as a theory. In interdisciplinary terms Bertalanffy thus thought that General Systems Theory would "… be methodologically an important means of controlling and investigating the transfer of principles from one field to another" and that his theory would "guard against superficial analogies, which are useless in science and harmful in their practical consequences." And the pre-condition of this would be the progressive unification of the sciences in the first place. Hence, the enterprise of Bertalanffy shows up as an inherently ethical and ecological project which also aims at increasing the awareness in every human of the need of being functionally interconnected with each other, with his or her community, with the whole of humanity, with the immediate terrestrial surroundings and with the biosphere. As a scientifically structured tool his approach may help to conceive, design and implement the research needed for allowing every scientist to develop his or her intuition and capabilities, for learning consistently to discover the laws that govern the manifestation of biological, psychological and social systems. It is the concept of *synergy* which Bertalanffy utilizes in order to express his conviction that there is a major organizing principle of the world whose understanding would in fact illuminate an appropriate ethics. And this is clearly where Bertalanffy meets Spinoza. What we will do here is to structure our viewpoints according to the tradition of which those two (among several others) have been outstanding protagonists, with all their insight and their errors as well, according to their own epoch and according to their individual state in the scientific community. Of course, we will not forget all the other main protagonists that also helped to shape what is *objective spirit* for us today.

****

This present text has gained a lot by the communicative discourse that characterizes daily life at a university, and I owe much to the kind interest and illuminating contributions provided by many colleagues and students who directly or indirectly added to the knowledge and understanding achieved thus far. Hence, I would like to thank all these persons for their support in one way or another, though I can only mention a few of them: In this sense, I thank the postdoc members and the PhD students of my group at the university of Kassel, notably Franziska Holzner, Carola Keitel, Annette Schlemm, Yvonne Thorhauer, and Doris Zeilinger for their activities relating to the various projects we could initiate during the last years. I also thank my students and doctorate students at the ICT&S at the university of Salzburg who were willing to get involved in the details of my lecture course that I gave during my stay as International Guest Professor there in the winter half year term of 2006/07. I would like to mention particularly those who contributed their papers to the recently published volume on the concept of harmony in urban space (Zimmermann, 2008d): Judith Gassner, Ulrike Hitzinger, Andreas Koller, Christoph Pranger, Celina Raffl, Matthias Schafranek, and Tomáš Sigmund. For the invitation to Salzburg I thank Wolfgang Hofkirchner, the head of the research group for *etheory* at the ICT&S, in the first place. I also thank his coworkers Christian Fuchs and Matthias Schafranek for helpful discussions on various aspects of the topics involved, and the staff of the ICT&S, notably Elke Holzmann, Hermann Huber, and Irina Véliz-Delgado, for the kind supervision and care during my stay. For helpfully providing a beautiful flat in Salzburg in walking distance to the institute, I thank Manfred Bayerl (Wien). During the final stage of translating the first volume of his epochal work on *The Method*, Edgar Morin (Paris) illuminated to me various aspects of his approach to the theory of evolutionary systems. I thank him very much for the clarifying and kind reaction to all my questions. For his interest and helpful comments concerning topoi I thank Yair Neuman (Beer Sheva). I also thank Paola Zizzi (Padova) for giving me the occasion to publish my viewpoints on the concept of emergence in physics. I also thank the two referees for valuable comments and suggestions.

CHAPTER 1

Introduction—Spinoza Today

In order to actually clarify the position taken by the philosophy of Spinoza as viewed in terms of a today's perspective, we have to look in some detail at the recently achieved state of philosophical knowledge. We will indeed discuss some of the aspects covered today by means of assuming a maximal consensus on the mainline of thinking rather than going into any more specialized approaches of philosophy. Hence, we will try to point to the role of Spinozist conceptions within a scenario which is essentially determined by what we call "systematic philosophy" as introduced by philosophers such as Schelling, Hegel, Marx, Bloch, Sartre and others on this same line of tradition. The idea is to demonstrate (very much in the sense of Theunissen) the impact of some kind of modernized metaphysics intrinsic to this aforementioned mainline thinking, in the sense that the theoretical nucleus of today's philosophy shows up as a suitable *ultima philosophia* of considerable heuristic value rather than the traditional *prima philosophia* in the Aristotelian sense as it had been intended in the first place. We propose here to visualize the philosophy of Spinoza as a suitable paradigm for such a required approach.

In order to do so we shortly summarize the following results formerly discussed at other places. In the past, we have elaborated somewhat on this topic. See in particular Zimmermann, 2002, 2004b. But the original paper discussing these topics within the context of modern physics is still Zimmermann, 2000. The latter however is only available as preprint file in the Los Alamos archive.

The main task of human beings is to model nature: To be more precise, they model their surrounding environment, and they model themselves within that environment. This serves them as a guideline for orientation within a complex world and gives them conceptions of how to actually deal with this world in practise. From what they have found out about the environment in their immediate vicinity, they infer results about phenomena and things which are far away—both in spatial and temporal terms, respectively. Hence, their epistemic idea is to generalize these results as far as possible; this *stabilizes experience* by means of the modeling done. Structurally stable aspects of nature can be taught then to others, because the models achieved imply general rules of and a systematic approach to nature which can be communicated easily. In principle then, teaching is a technique of "saving experience".

At the same time, humans are also a *product* of nature. That is, they have emerged from the same process they are trying to model in the first place. By having been produced, they now interact with nature in order to actively modify it according to their objectives. They are thus participators rather than mere observers. In so far as they are nature's product, their modifying of nature is still nothing but the same process representing nature's activity. Hence, in principle, nature is actually modifying *itself* by means of human (research) activities.

Obviously, the various fields of scientific activity are divided according to the "regional" aspects nature is displaying for the various perspectives of systematic interest. The division of labour is also applied to "research labour" in the sense that it reduces the observed complexity of the world. In fact, thinking itself is deeply rooted in this permanent activity of reducing complexity. By doing so, humans think in a "digital" rather than analogous way, that is they artificially introduce sections and intervals, or distances into the process they actually observe—they "sequentialize" this process which remains however all the time quite an analogous (continuous) process, if viewed in terms of human perception and/or cognition. On the other hand, modern physics, e.g., tends to show that space is intrinsically *digitalized* in a way, and so might be time. And this specialized result would not come as a surprise, in fact, because one would expect that human research means—given that human beings are products of nature—that the models gained become more and more adapted to a realistic world view (whatever this may be). Hence, the apparent contradiction between continuous and discrete structures of the world leading to different concepts of process has always been very much in the centre of discussion. Although the modeling performed introduces a level of abstraction into nature which seems to lead away from concrete, practical nature, it is nevertheless nearer to reality in the sense that humans may learn to differentiate between how the world appears to be in its *modality* and how it may actually be in its *reality*.

Unfortunately, this idea also precludes the possibility that humans might ever be able to actually recognize the world as it really is: In other words, humans perceive the world according to their biological constitution which is itself an outcome of the process of nature and is moreover modeled as such by humans themselves. The point is that these means of perception opening up a way to cognitively grasp the world are aimed towards optimizing orientation within the practical world (e.g., for being able to find enough food or being protected). But there is no reason to believe that there is any necessity involved in a fitting of these perceptive capacities to the actual uncovering of the real structure of the world. Without any doubt, there *is* some real world of which humans are a part, and obviously, it *can* be mapped adequately in one way or the other, but this does not tell us of any kind of absolute truth about the being of the world.

(In fact, there is nothing or nobody non-human in nature that/who cares about human knowledge. Evolution is always neutral.)

In a sense, the speculative abilities of human reflexion can be visualized as a kind of excess knowledge achieved—probably because the impetus of striving for insight possesses a kind of dynamical space of free play which within the field of its anticipations opens up considerably the pathway to more possibilities than are actually needed for the time being. The explicit *topics* of speculation however, as well as the topics of empirical research have not really changed, because, given the human relation to environment, the choice is probably limited.

The traditional division of scientific fields, having actually been developed by Stoic philosophers for the first time within a European context in all generality, about 2300 years ago, has remained essentially invariant until today, though the utilized terminology and the conceptual attitude might have changed considerably. In the sense of this original Stoic terminology, *physics* is dealing with the modeling of non-human nature, *logic* with the modeling of the thinking about (modeling) nature, and *hermeneutic* with the modeling of thinking about thinking (We do impose here a mild reductionism in using epistemological core categories rather than fields of research. In this sense, the sciences become *reducible* to physics such that the latter is always included in all of them as a special case at their basic foundations. But higher levels of complexity are *irreducible* to physics in the sense that by passing down the hierarchy, emergent properties are effectively being lost. And because of humans being a product of nature, their models of nature must necessarily contain *self-models*. In fact, it appears to be reasonable to assume that each model of nature contains at least one self-model. We have discussed this in more detail in Zimmermann, 1988).

So we may come to the conclusion that all this modeling going on is primarily one of a unified character, because it is dealing with a unified whole, a totality which cannot actually be broken up into parts, if not accepting that important information will be lost then. On the other hand, because of practical reasons, it is not possible to model everything at the same time. (Even the celebrated *theory of everything* in physics would be only a theory of everything in physics after all.) Hence, humans have to take into account both of these aspects: They have to study the minute details of nature, but they have also to think about the interactive pattern which is constituting nature's totality, of which they are actually a part themselves by performing their research activities. For the one task they do possess the sciences which deal with a fragment of nature only, according to the definitions of their "regional competence", for which they are designed in the first place, and according to their thus prescribed boundaries (which are sometimes rather fluid though nowadays). The problem with this approach is that very often, research in one field is not at all related to or even knows of research in another so that the possible interactions of these fragments are more or less lost. That is why philosophy takes the other perspective and centres around the aspect of totality. In doing so, philosophy today has developed as a *science of the sciences*, or as a science of totality, following up the scientific results given at a time, rather than trying to lay the grounds for science, as it has been the tradition for a long time. Contrary to what was intended by the Aristotelian idea of "prima philosophia", philosophy is now putting forward research of a more conceptual and heuristic kind (we have referred to this aspect earlier in more detail in Zimmermann, 1999).

Given these preliminary reflexions we will try to show now that the philosophy of Spinoza can actually serve as a characteristic paradigm for a line of thinking which generically ends up with what we have mentioned before. In the next chapter we will show then how this relates to the modern development of a theory of evolutionary systems. We will argue that nowadays, such a theory is the best possible approach towards an "ultima philosophia" of the aforementioned kind. And we will realize that philosophy today—but nevertheless a philosophy which moves in the strict tradition of Spinoza's—is not only a science (of the sciences) by mere name, but also one which can be formalized and tested and which can make both conceptualization and heuristic proposition concrete.

****

As it turns out, Spinoza had already thought of most of the aforementioned aspects: For a long time, the consequent resumption and continuation of the Stoic line of thought had been obstructed due to ideological reasons, especially with a view to the dynamical aspects of nature primarily based on an active principle of self-creation leading forward to the possibility of the concept of field with respect to physical forces. Ironically however, it was exactly this sort of negative approach which in the fashion of a mere by-product made it possible to gain more insight into the relationship between the world and its foundation in the long run, because the contradictions actually encountered sooner or later did not leave another way out than just that very resumption of the Stoic line. The permanent spinning around the relationship between God and the world ended finally in blind alleys and on wrong tracks. But their by-passing in terms of modern (Renaissance) mathematics opened up an alternative approach with a two-fold result: On the one hand, the ancient concept of substance was re-formulated in an abstract way, in explicitly denying its existence in the traditional, scholastic sense, but at the same time re-introducing it as a concept in terms of a productive misunderstanding and in a somewhat clandestine way. On the other hand, the progressing detachment of philosophy from theology opened up a new route to all aspects of nature which had been suppressed before: in particular, the aspect of a dynamical, self-creative and self-organizing matter as substratum and potential of an unfolding nature, including a re-definition of the organizational hierarchy of the Universe, and of the mediation of matter with its explicit forms up to its social forms constituting human systems, themselves dealing with the reflexion of this very process, being subjected however to incomplete information. So it was left to Spinoza after all to actually draw all these aspects together again and to re-base them onto a sound foundation of Stoic systematics, at the same time giving a modern terminology to them which is still relevant for us today.

But Spinoza does not only cumulate the various strings of the philosophy of his time in order to transform them into an inherently Stoic form. He also visualizes philosophy as something which is practically identical with ethics. For him, philosophy is a theory of the conditions according to which human life is being defined. And this definition can only be rational, if it is coupled to an ethical frame of references. Ethics itself then, unfolds the conditions according to which the human striving can be realized. Humans are capable in this sense, of finding and conserving their own mode of being, if they act according to adequate knowledge. Hence, there is a close connection between freedom and insight. It is necessary therefore, to find adequate ways (*inveniri*) in an appropriate project which is to be designed by humans themselves. If Spinoza's "Ethics" (throughout the text we use the English notation when referring to the "Ethics", the first number giving the part, the letter referring to the state of the proposition, in a somewhat self-explanatory manner, the second number following the usual listing of propositions) states (in 1p34) that the power of God is his own *essence* (*Dei potentia est ipsa ipsius essentia*), then, for humans, one could add that (in an existential sense) the power of humans is their own *existence* (*Humani potentia est ipsa ipsius existentia*). And the adequate form of this existence is being prescribed in terms of the virtue which leads forward to blissful happiness. For humans therefore, virtue in this sense and power, are identical (4d8) (Although, for reasons of simplicity, we keep "power" here for Spinoza's expression "potentia", it should be noted that "potential" (in the sense of capacity, ability, …), in contrary to "potestas" (power) is certainly a better translation. In so far we follow here the opinion of the English translator of Antonio Negri's book on Spinoza: The Savage Anomaly, University of Minnesota Press, Minneapolis, Oxford, 1991 [= *L'anomalia selvaggia: Saggio su potere e potenza* in Baruch Spinoza, 1981]. In Italian, there is a generic difference between the two expressions as indicated in the title (potere, potenza). The same is true for French (pouvoir, puissance). We claim this difference also for German (Macht, Vermoegen). See the translator's remarks in: Negri, 1991: xi sqq.). This is not only a mere re-formulation of Stoic ideas, but Spinoza also tries to define substance (God = nature) as *causa immanens* of the world, but in terms of a twofold perspective taken according to whether the relationship between God and the world is visualized under the substantial (real) perspective of God himself, or under the modal perspective of humans who represent a finite mode of what worldly exists. Indeed, the former perspective can be taken in speculative terms only, but because God represents himself completely in each of his attributes, it is possible that humans can grasp his (i.e., substance's) existence *in principle* at least, provided they have developed the adequate knowledge about this due to their adequate reflexion. In this sense, everything is in God (*quicquid est, in Deo est*), but the vice versa is also true.

On the other hand, reflexion itself is an outcome of the organization of substance: The constitution of the latter according to which it is productive with respect to the field of modi, is its organization in terms of attributes (Bartuschat, 1992: 66 gives a precise discussion of this aspect). This means that God does not really produce attributes, but he as substance is *attributively organized* instead. Hence, God is *causa sui* only in so far as he produces everything what there is, but this is only true with respect to the finite perspective of humans.

Nevertheless, a finite mode is in God, because it is a created mode within the totality of nature. But in this mode as its cause, it is only God who acts as immanent cause of permanency, it is not however the totality of nature which acts as this cause (Bartuschat, 1992: 44-49 (par.)). Hence, nature has to be discussed in different terms as compared to substance. Spinoza classifies nature according to an earlier viewpoint of Averroes (Ibn Rushd): He actually differs between *natura naturans* (the actively creating nature producing the worldly) and *natura naturata* (the passively produced nature which is the outcome of the performance of natura naturans). The former represents God's own productivity, the latter its (observed) result. *Hence, nature is the form of mediation in which God acts upon the world as seen and interpreted under the modal perspective of humans.* Note however that God does not think himself, because it is only the humans who do (2a2). And therefore, God is not a spirit either (Bartuschat, 1992: 65).

So nature has an important role to play within the frame of references which constitutes the world. But as it is only humans that think, the basic concept of worldly orientation is (human communicative) *intersubjectivity* in the first place, nature only in second. It is thus reflexion, and it is *the political form of communication* that determine adequate knowledge. The latter can only be achieved, if the structure of the world in terms of its nature is uncovered and logically displayed. Hence, to study nature means to lay the ground for adequate knowledge, and in the end, for adequate *action* according to ethical principles. And this is a holistic viewpoint indeed.

In a way, Spinoza follows the Cartesian approach of deducing physics from metaphysics (1988: 39). But he is far more radical than Descartes. Gabriel Albiac (1997: 127sq.) has expressed this clearly: "... nothing happens in Nature ... The conclusion imposes itself. It is only within the framework of a general theory of Nature that there will be room to understand all things (human or other) that it contains. [Hence], ... the *Ethics* ... is a physics, which is a metaphysics." Spinoza himself mentions this aspect in a letter to Blijenbergh when he speaks of an "... Ethics, which, as everyone knows, must be founded on metaphysics and physics..." (Quoted according to Gabbey, 1996: 184n.18). He seeks to derive his ethical theory from this basic understanding of nature in the first place, the psychology of humans showing up within this framework as *human nature*, a particular case of nature in general. *In this sense, every human action must be conceived as a manifestation of nature* (Garrett, 1996: 270).

Note that this also refers to the celebrated aspect of determinism in Spinoza, but not as we know it: Instead of "determinism" it would be more adequate to speak of "necessitarianism", because nature is actually determining behavior, but in an intrinsically contingent way. Hence, there is always a sufficient reason for everything what happens, and a kind of causal closure (consistency), but there is not necessarily a fixed "program" of given processes. (As we would say today, physics is certainly determining the laws of events taking place in the arena of the world, because "everything is basically physics"—but this insight is completely unsatisfactory without having done the difficult work, too: namely the reconstructing of the various levels of the hierarchy of complexity and their mediation towards the phenomena actually being observed. This solves, by the way, the problem of determinism as to human decisions: Because human cognition depends on sensory perception, the information collected before deciding something is always incomplete. In other words: Everyday decision of humans depends on observable data which are emergent with respect to the essentially unobservable processes actually taking place. Hence, even agreed that the latter determine behavior, action is free in the sense that humans have always the choice. (And they *have* the choice, because they can never know for certain.)

All of this has a decisive consequence for the *praxis* visualized as human existence: For Spinoza, the striving for conserving one's own being (*conatus in suo esse perseverandi*) can be interpreted in terms of an ethics which unfolds the conditions under which this striving can actually be realized. Under them, therefore, the individual human being can indeed arrive at his/her *eigen-being* (Bartuschat, 1992: x, see also 186, (referring to 4p18), 200. (This has also strong Sartrean connotations, because such a human can be easily visualized as one "who is able to become what he/she actually is".) Provided he/she applies what Spinoza calls the *true method* consisting of "the knowledge alone of the pure understanding, of its nature and of its laws. To acquire this method, you must first of all distinguish between intellect and imagination, or between true ideas and the others, that is fictitious / false and doubtful ideas, and, absolutely speaking, all those that depend on memory alone" (Gabbey, 1996: 171sq. He refers to the epistle 37 to Bouwmeester).

Hence, this is the kind of "ideal of a unified science" (Curley, 1988: 4,6, also title of ch. 1 sect. 2) Spinoza is aiming at. In principle, he seeks primarily to improve the character of human beings by improving their self-understanding. And he justifies this with the argument that it would bring humans the ultimate peace of mind as (being) integral aspects of nature. Garrett notes that Spinoza, very much like Hobbes, conceives of human beings as "mechanisms in nature" that are motivated by self-preservation and individual advantage. *They can improve their way of life by the mutual employment of reason.* Hobbes however, tries to show how humans can optimize the chances for a good life by instituting political constraints on their passions. Spinoza's aim is far more ambitious: He sets out to show how humans can achieve a way of life that largely transcends the mere transitory desires leading to an autonomous control over passions (Garrett, 1996: 267sq. (par.))

It is in this way that Spinoza's monistic and naturalistic system speaks "most cogently and persuasively to the twentieth century" (Garrett in his introduction to the Cambridge Companion, 2). In fact, it is doing so by explicating three basic aspects which have become very important for modern research in recent times:

1. Visualizing a transcendental materialism with physics "at the bottom";
2. A radical approach to interdisciplinarity, and;
3. Aiming at mediations leading up to ethics and politics. As far as physics is concerned Spinoza writes to Tschirnhaus:

> *By physics I understand nothing else than the science of the universe demonstrated a priori by the rigorous method of the mathematicians and confirmed a posteriori by the most evident experiences which even convince the imagination ... This science is truly divine. One here exposes the laws ... according to which everything produces invariably its effects. The knowledge of this science liberates us also of innumerable prejudices ... In this way, through the mediation of the true physics, one becomes so to say a completely new man and one is regenerated philosophically ... Ultimately,* thanks to physics *we are prepared for still more important knowledge* (quoted according to Klever, 1996: 52)

Hence, the program of the "Ethics" is one which confirms our view today as we have introduced it in the beginning: the first point being to know our own nature as good as possible, desiring to perfect it, and the second being to know as much of the nature of things as is necessary (Klever, 1996: 53).

But this radical kind of interdisciplinarity is also very much on our presently modern line of thinking: Spinoza's necessitarianism (being based on a firm view of an ontological monism) leads him to abolish the classical divisions of *prudentiae* and *scientiae* "making the principal subjects of the Ethics and the two political Treatises formal impossibilities within a Peripatetic perspective." (Gabbey, 1996: 148, referring to 1p29) This is what Negri actually means when speaking of Spinoza as "anomaly": "Spinoza is the anomaly. The fact that Spinoza, atheist and damned, does not end up behind bars or burned at the stake, ... can only mean that his metaphysics effectively represents the pole of an antagonistic relationship of force that is already solidly established: The development of productive forces and relations of production in seventeenth-century Holland already comprehends the tendency toward an antagonistic future"(Negri, 1991: XVII, preface).

Hence, in his striving for an *experientia sive praxis* (Negri, 1991: 183 (section title)) Spinoza aims at a theory of the world, beginning with physics, ending up with social systems, proposing educational means of eventually approaching a state which, in an equilibrium of the individual and the institution, harmonizes human spirit in order to let it participate in the larger harmony which is expressed in the material attribute of godly substance. Quite obviously, this is the reason for the recent reception of Spinoza's in explicitly Marxist terms, notably in Althusser. It is Tosel in fact, who recognizes an ethico-political consequence emerging from Spinoza's approach, basing it on definite materialistic philosophemes and a collection of motives generic for Marxist theory: "*L'onto-théologie est éthico-politique: Dieu, c'est-à-dire la légalité d'une Nature immanente, se traduit humainement dans l'immanence d'une société rationellement réglée d'hommes capables de penser et agir. Et l'éthico-politique est à son tour ontologique : L'homme libre est une possibilité de la nature anonyme*" (Tosel, 1994: 18. "The onto-theology is ethico-political: God, i.e., the legality of an immanent nature, translates itself into the immanence of a society which is rationally regulated by humans who are able to think and to act. And the ethico-political is, on the other hand, ontological: The free human being is a possibility of anonymous nature"—our translation).

He lists then a number of appropriate philosophemes: Nothing comes from nothing(ness)—*ex nihilo nihil fit*—everything has a reason which can be illuminated by its foundation in terms of possibility, the real has objectivity which can be illuminated by science, hence, philosophy is also scientific and deals with the fundamental structures of what there is, dealing also with itself, in order to produce knowledge about itself and about human thinking in general, hence, philosophy-science determines itself as a science of humans, being based on the fundamental thesis that humans are themselves nature, not an empire within an empire, *this science of humans is scientific ethics*, that is re-organization and re-orientation of human life (Tosel, 1994: 132, par.).

In this sense, Tosel shows that for Spinoza, all of (actual) reality emerges from another reality which is basically material, and the unity of which is immanent in the variety, and coincides with its own space of productivity. Hence, cosmology, physics, and logic are the basic fields for constituting anthropology (Tosel, 1994: 133, 135, par.).

This leads in a straightforward way to all those topics which are of considerable interest for us today, when we try to find a new synthesis of philosophy, the sciences, and the arts on the one hand, and daily praxis on the other. And we can realize the strong existentialistic connotation being handed down to us from Spinoza: Because philosophy is as it is, it has also a fundamental interest in the liberating of humans. In other words: Philosophy aims to a positive liberty of individuals against all kinds of heteronomy. Philosophy is thus a theory and a praxis of autonomy at the same time. And finally, in being a science of humans, philosophy is also an instrument of critique, i.e., *it is criticizing especially all authorities which do not base their principles on communicative arguments*. Research about life is therefore research of (and about) *free* life in the first place, of a life which has no other generic principle than its physico-psychic unity. For this, nature is the original reality, and as such this nature is intelligible, and it is anterior to all thinking (Tosel, 1994: 187sq., 190, par.).

In recent times, the approaching of Spinoza by means of a political theory has been discussed in detail following the publication of the books by Antonio Negri and Michael Hardt (Hardt & Negri, 2000, 2004). In particular, the concepts of "empire" and "multitude" are directly derived from Spinoza's works. Going back to the original conception of Spinoza's we notice a primary basic idea which is also inherent in the works of Negri and Hardt. (See in more detail Fuchs, Zimmermann, 2008. We follow here the exposition in this book when discussing Spinoza's political ideas.)

Essentially, the leading line of argument points to the two-sided implication of two identities which do not necessarily appear to be mutually compatible in the first place:

$$virtus = potentia \Leftrightarrow civitas = multitudo$$

In the terminology of Spinoza, this implicational formula interrelates the concepts of "virtue" and "potential" on the one hand, "citizenry" and "multitude" on the other. The respective identities of the two pairs of concepts however (always understood in terms of being a postulated ideal and thus an ethical demand rather than a concrete situation) cause various difficulties, because their realization in terms of practical daily life seems counter-intuitive and not quite a straightforward operation of illustrating an idealized principle. The underlying problem is in fact one of mediation: This is so because the implication's identity on the left-hand side refers to individual persons while the identity on the right-hand side refers to (social) groups of persons. Hence, any practical realization of the inferred principle should operate on two different levels which are dialectically mediated, and this turns out to be the most difficult problem of any ethical approach. (In fact, as it appears, this may also pose a serious problem for the approach offered by Negri and Hardt, because making the multitude topical is only one half of the task, and perhaps it is thus that the latter's ideas appear a little abstract from time to time.)

Spinoza himself anticipated this difficulty and appealed to human reason: In the fourth part of his "Ethics" (Of Human Bondage) he writes that a person who strives for a good, will also demand this good for other people the more he/she participates in the knowledge of God (4p37). And in the second note (scholium) to that proposition he adds that it is necessary to achieve a unification of the multitude of the many within politics *by means of reason*: "It is necessary therefore that humans in order to be able to live in concord with one another and be helpful to each other give up their natural right and secure not to do anything in future which would impair others" (4p37s2—our translation). As it turns out the problem is deeply buried in the anticipation of the above proposition: To assume that a good is also something which is to be desired for all others is not only an idealistic conjecture, but poses the most central problem of ethics, until today, even after the illuminated approach by French existentialism (Zimmermann, 2002a). As Spinoza has a theory of state contracts and laws in mind, he might have been too rash to assume some sort of ontological altruism where there is only the wish for individual security.

Spinoza is more precise as to his point when discussing the state in his Political Tractatus [PT henceforth] where he defines a perspective in terms of natural law such that common laws imply a restriction of personal rights according to the individual potential available. Spinoza continues that hence, nobody has any right beyond what is granted to him/her by common law (PT II, § 16) (We refer here to Spinoza, 1994). In other words: *Common law is nothing but coercion after all, because it is primarily a constraint.* So in order to demand a good (and to assume that it is also a good for others) entails to accept that the others do not share this assumption. This is exactly what Spinoza means when talking of the multitude: "This right [to dissent from the individual] which is defined by the potential [power] of the crowd [multitudo] is usually called sovereignty of the state, if visualized as power of government. It is completely subjected to the person who is in charge of the state administration *out of a common consent* … Is this the task of an assembly which is constituted out of the whole crowd [multitudo] we call the state 'democracy'…" (PT II, §17—our emphasis).

Wolfgang Bartuschat discusses this point in more detail in his introduction to the German edition of the *Political Tractatus*. He refers back to the "Ethics" (2p13) where Spinoza speaks about physical bodies. Bartuschat argues that models of that kind cannot be applied to a theory of the state, because humans would not be primarily bodies but also spiritual beings (because they possess a mind) (Bartuschat, in Spinoza, 1994: xvi-xvii). However, this argument is not valid anymore, because we would visualize today mind as a special case of the attribute of matter—and in fact, it is likely that Spinoza himself did not find this too alien (Zimmermann, 2000). If in particular, we visualize the world (as perceived under the attribute of matter) as a self-organized system constituted by agent systems, as we do in some more recent theories, then the state is either no artefact or the Universe is (Zimmermann, 2007b, d).

Implicitly however, Bartuschat agrees with that, even under the perspective of Spinoza: He mentions (Bartuschat, in Spinoza, 1994: xxiv-xxv) that Spinoza defines the right derived from the sovereignty of the state simply as the right which is constituted by the power (potential) of the crowd (multitudo), as we have seen above. But he also notes that while "multitudo" is the name of the actual unity of all people representing the common power of all the individuals (combined), it is not shown that such a power is possible at all. For him, this is only true for a state whose supreme power is in fact the power of the crowd. Hence, we circle around a problem of the state. In a sense, such a state is something which is still in the future, is actually *hoped for* (with Blochian connotations here and hence with a somewhat utopian quality). Spinoza is optimistic in the sense that he argues in favour of such a state, because as a natural object, it strives for self-preservation, and thus creates laws in order to secure this. So in the end, there is (for Spinoza as visualized within the interpretation of Bartuschat's) a fundamental sort of agency acting!

We have here the right-hand side of the above identity implication: Provided we had such a state, then all the fear would vanish, all the citizens would be integrated in the procedures of creating laws such that they could understand these laws as their own laws, and thus they would not have to fear them anymore. This would be indeed the real achievement of the identity of *multitudo* and *civitas* within the concept of common power (Bartuschat, in Spinoza, 1994: xxvii-xxix).

However, there remains the problem of concrete practibility: Bartuschat continues that an unrestricted form of government would be one which is controlled by the crowd itself such that the power which is issuing the laws does not act against groups which have to fear it as long as they themselves are not integrated into the process of creating law (Bartuschat, in Spinoza, 1994: xxxiii; cf. PT VIII, 3). This is the real problem: Does integration in that sense already entail interiorization of common power for the group in question?

In his first book on Spinoza, Negri starts indeed from this juridical point of view. The important formulation is here: "*Civil Right is the power [potentia] of the multitude.*" (Negri, 1991: 195—our emphasis). This actually demonstrates that the constitution of collectivity as praxis has to precede the process of constituting civil right. In other words, we have to invoke the left-hand side of the aforementioned identity implication again in order to gain an understanding of the right-hand side which is topical in the discussion about the state: "We must not, therefore, look to the precepts of reason [*ex rationis documentis*] for the causes and natural foundations of the State, but derive them from the common nature or condition of mankind."(TP I, 7 as quoted in Negri, 1991: 189). Hence, the *struggle of power [potentia] against Power [potestas]* is in fact defining for the problem in question (Negri, 1991: 196). After all, this struggle mirrors another struggle: that of the right-hand side against the left-hand side of our identity implication. A human state system is very much posed on the "edge of chaos": "The best constitution is posed ... on the limit between civil right and the right to war: Freedom is made from the first right, and peace from the second" (Negri, 1991: 201).

The foundation therefore comes from the "common nature" of humans *within nature*. (This is indeed conformal with Spinoza's approach which is also based on the explication of an immanent nature.) As Balibar states: "Thus, every *populus* is the continuous regulation of the relation that the powers [potentiae] of the multitude maintain with nature of which they form a part..." (Balibar 1997: 184).

Negri shows that essentially, Spinoza follows his approach already laid down in the Theological-political Tractatus (Negri 1997: 220sq., 231). Here, the concept of "multitudo" however, although being immanent, has not yet acquired an explicitly political dimension. But also here, the life of absolute government is endowed with a systole and diastole and operates on the edge of chaos (Negri, 1997: 229sq.). In theological terms it is here the place where the concept of *pietas* is being asked for as the desire that no subject be excluded from universality. (Nowadays we can notice, as visualized within a more political framework, that this is indeed a concept which can be usefully applied to work in daily life.) As Negri points out this is something different from any condition of mere equality which is not objective of the given project (Negri, 1999: 316). Utilizing ethics as a critical method rather than a list of purported results means that this concept of (Spinozist) ethics is near to that of Sartre and Kristeva (Negri. 1999: 321sq.). Consequently, in their book on the multitude, Hardt and Negri (2004) point to models which assume creative agents and complex networks, leaving open a space of free play in which the self-reference of social systems may be able to productively unfold.

Which also implies the immanence of virtualities and utopian non-locations: It is not a coincidence that Hardt and Negri use the now fashionable concept of "matrix" in order to characterize the structure of social systems (Hardt & Negri, 2004: 335sq.). Indeed, in their book on the empire (Hardt & Negri, 2000), the category of the possible has its place within the context of virtuality and what they call the circulation of space (Hardt & Negri, 2000: 365, 404. In fact, critique applied to this approach can usually be easily refuted: see, e.g., Marin Terpstra (Terpstra, 1994) or Bartuschat (1992: 237). In particular, with a view to Hegel and Marx and their reception of Spinoza see Christopher Norris (1991: 21-53). Here again, agents are prominent (Norris, 1991: 45) and the concept of a "theoretical praxis" (in the sense of Bourdieu) (Norris, 1991: 49). See also very illuminating altogether Yirmiyahu Yovel, 1994/1989).

Note that within this framework it becomes quite clear that the well-known Hegelian critique concerning Spinoza's approach is rather dispensable, especially with a view to the concrete topicality of social antagonisms and conflicts in Spinoza which Hegel is obviously unable to detect. Moreover, as to the systematic structure of Spinoza's approach (in both ontological as well as epistemological terms), we have to correct a number of points which are always subject to misunderstandings and errors of interpretation, which should be clarified somewhat before we enter further discussion. Hence, we will shortly summarize aspects of the role of space, the celebrated identity theorem of the second part of the "Ethics", and semiotic details which can be derived therefrom.

First of all, we will look at the relation between substance and the fundamental categories of space and time: Essentially, the attribute of extension can be visualized as space itself (we follow here explicitly the much plausible exposition in Bennett, 1996: 69). Hence, the actual difference between the approaches of Spinoza and Leibniz can be phrased then in terms of the relationship between (observable) objects and space: Leibniz explains away the region and stays with the relations among bodies, taking the region as an alternative way of expressing facts about them. Spinoza explains away the objects and stays with the region. Referring to a famous example, Bennett formulates: "If there is (…) a pebble in region R, what makes this true is the fact that R is *pebbly* [which] stands for a certain monadic property that a spatial region / can have. If the pebble moves (…), what makes this true is the fact that there is a continuous change in which regions are pebbly: The so-called movement of a pebble through space is like the so-called movement of a panic through a crowd" (Bennett, 1996: 70sq.). (Note that this offers a relatively clear explanation of how we should visualize *motion-in-itself* which is still a topic in Hegel.) But then, time does not remain a fundamental category itself: Spinoza states in his 12th letter that "… *tempus* [is] nothing but a mode of the imagination which ought to mean that in a true fundamental account of the whole of reality th[is] concept … would not be used. [Hence,] all our measures—of time and space and of things spatial and temporal—are superficial and "imaginative", and not part of the basic, objective story." (Bennett, 1996: 77, also referring to 1p15s). Although essentially, this conception is widely agreed upon, at the same time, it has been the target of many controversies (see, e.g., the comments of Juhani Peitarinen to our Helsinki paper in Eeva Matikainen (ed.)(2002). It can be easily shown however that Spinoza ties time to imagination (2p44s) when basically referring it to human (sensory) perceptions of varying motions of bodies (cf. Wilson, 1996: 139 n. 51). Hence, temporality actually emerges in the transition from infinity to finite modes (of thinking) as laid down in the "Ethics" (2p8 and its corollary) (Bartuschat, in Spinoza, 1994: 85). In fact, as Bartuschat mentions explicitly in his discussion at this point, the corollary has the important function of marking the transition to finite modes, and it is here where Spinoza actually changes his perspective of description in the "Ethics" (Bartuschat, in Spinoza (1994: 85). Also van Zandt, 1986: 256, agrees with this stating: "… [d]uration, then, is solely to be found in Natura naturata …" It is not clear however why he relates this result to considering the space-time manifold "as a whole" to "eternal natura naturans" (van Zandt, 1986: 257, 259). Ironically enough, when Kouznetsov once referred to quantum theory as representing natura naturans, he was not so far off as Paty thinks in his article following van Zandt's, cf. Paty (1986) with a view to Kouznetsov (1967)).

Obviously, if temporality is part of the human world in modal terms, then there is no problem of determinism. But still, the question is as to the actual structure of the human mode of being which is also the human mode of perception (and as such includes both space and time). The main theorem around which this question circles is in fact Spinoza's identity theorem (2p7). If indeed "… thought is coextensive with materiality…" (Wilson, 1996: 115), then the ethical implications of Spinoza rest basically on the fact that human thinking is not a mere passive reflexion of the body's vicissitudes: "As well as being mapped onto a segment of the material world, the mind is inserted into the totality of thought" (Lloyd, 1994: 27). Hence, a singular individual is not a self which also strives for something, but a singular individual is a *self-in-striving*, and it possesses an explicit *project structure* (very much in the sense of modern existential philosophy). But this project which in the end shows up as the dynamical core of existence, is a representation of the human's finite mode of being which points toward the adequate form of knowledge humans can have, because it is this knowledge in which they actually conserve their own being. And the generic form of realizing existence is *acting* according to the results of adequate reflexion (Bartuschat, in Spinoza, 1994: xi, 132sq.)

So, human reflexion means nothing else but explicating the symbolic traces in existence which intrinsically point to the true mediation of what there is with substance, visualized in terms of the latter's attributes. Modeling the world in human terms means thus modeling the configuration of worldly attributes. The latter however cannot be modeled without modeling its foundation (substance) at the same time. This is the point where *sceptical* philosophy is clearly based and dependent on *speculative* philosophy. In fact, human reflexion has the actual task of organizing the infinite (Negri, 1997: 52) by means of the finite. And both of them are "knotted to each other" in terms of the consequences of the aforementioned identity theorem (2p7): "Mental items can be mapped onto bodily items in a way that preserves causal connectedness." (This is an alternative formulation of Bennett's (1996: 78). In other words: If M is the category of mental states (whose objects are the states and whose morphisms are changes of states), and if B is the category of bodily states (whose objects are the states and whose morphisms are changes of states), respectively, then there is a functor $B \Rightarrow M$ preserving identities and compositions of morphisms (We come back to the language of mathematical categories later. Note first that the original formulation of the theorem (*Ordo & connexio idearum idem est, ac ordo & connexio rerum.*) does not imply equality of mental and bodily states, but only an isomorphism of changes of states. In so far, the further discussion in Bennett (1996: 79) is not quite clear). *This relationship secures that humans are actually capable at all of adequately interpreting the symbolic traces intrinsic to the world they observe.* And this is the reason why speculative philosophy is of heuristic importance for research.

As to a possible semiological re-construction of this concept of symbolic traces in Spinoza, Deleuze has given a classification of signs which are relevant for the understanding of this mediative structure of the world (Deleuze, 1997, see also Deleuze, 1968). He introduces four principal types of scalar signs, and two types of vectorial signs, in the following manner: *Scalar* signs are of *indicative* type according to whether they deal with sensory or perceptive physical effects, indicating human nature rather than anything else, of *abstractive* type according to whether human nature, being finite, retains some selected characters from what affects it, of *imperative* type according to whether effects are taken for ends, or ideas of effects for causes, actually producing moral effects, and finally of *hermeneutic* type according to whether humans imagine supra-sensible beings as an enlarged image of what effects them. Hence, these types of signs define sensible indices, logical icons, moral symbols, and metaphysical idols, respectively.

Vectorial signs can be identified with affects and are basically of an *augmentative* type, if they carry positive connotations, or of a *diminuitive* type, if they carry negative connotations. The common characteristics of all these signs are associability, variability, and equivocality or analogy. (The question arises whether this can be carried further by applying properties of mathematical categories.) In particular, the vectorial signs can be combined in their effect in order to define explicit gradients of social fields (Deleuze, 1997: 22sq.).

Deleuze also points out that "[if] signs, like words, are conventional, it is precisely because they act on natural signs and simply classify their variability and equivocity: conventional signs are abstractions that fix a relative constant for variable chains of association. Signs do not have objects as their direct referent. They are states of bodies (affections) and variations of power (affects) each of which refer to the other. Signs refer to signs" (Deleuze, 1997: 23). Thus signs are also effects, and effects refer to effects as signs to signs. They are actually "… consequences separated from their premises." Deleuze uses here an optical metaphor: "Effects or signs are *shadows* that play on the surface of bodies. The shadow is always on the border. It is always a body that casts a shadow on another… Signs are *effects of light* in a space filled with things colliding into each other at random" (Deleuze, 1997: 24).

In Spinoza, the determining oppositions to signs are common notions or concepts. They are primarily based on structures, and modes are geometric but fluid structures that are permanently being transformed. Hence, structure is also rhythm, that is, the linking of figures that compose and de-compose their relations. In this sense, modes can be visualized as projections of light: "Or rather, the variations of an object are projections that *envelop* a relation of movement and rest as their invariant (involution)" (Deleuze, 1997: 24sq.). In a sense, they are also colors or coloring causes: "Colors enter into relations of complementarity and contrast, which means that each of them, at the limit, re-constitutes the whole, and that they all merge together in whiteness (infinite mode) following an order of composition, or stand out from it in the order of de-composition" (Deleuze, 1997: 25). Hence, the whole "Ethics" can be read in terms of the scholia which constitute a book of signs "… which never ceases to accompany the more visible *Ethics*, the book of the concept…" (Deleuze, 1997: 28). Signs and affects, or concepts, shall be transgressed in the end, by arriving at essences or singularities, percepts. No longer signs of shadow or of light as color is important then, but light *in itself and for itself* (Deleuze, 1997: 30). Hence, the adequate form of re-flexion required here is simply a hermeneutic approach to nature. For eventually achieving this, the actual transition from logic to hermeneutic must be based on the space of free play which is intrinsic to the mediation of world and substance, modal and real existence, as it is characterized by the parallelism which can be represented in mathematical terms. (This is an aspect which practically unifies the ontological and epistemological domains.)

For Spinoza therefore, substance is what is in-itself and what can only be comprehended by itself and out of itself. This means that it is something whose concept does not need the concept of anything else in order to be formed. Hence, substance is its own reason (*causa sui*), and its essence involves its own existence. But humans, being a finite mode of this infinite substance, can only perceive their world in terms of attributes of that substance. In fact, their world is defined in terms of these attributes of which there are infinitely many, of which humans however can only perceive the two which fall into their mode of being: matter (*res extensa*) and mind (*res cogitans*). Note that not only is the world not the same as substance, but humans are also permanently modeling the attri-butes in a kind of recursive approximation, rather than perceiving them as they actually are once and for all. Hence, the relationship between the real perspec-tive of substance and the modal perspective of humans is difficult to visualize and poses problems: Although e.g., the infinite substance is undivisable (has no parts), humans actually perceive parts of objects in terms of the attributes of substance, but this is only a modal phenomenon and not a fact in real terms (cf. 1p15s).

So for humans, substance is the foundation of being, and as such it is *non-being*. It is not nothing(ness), because the world, as visualized in modal terms, has eventually emerged from substance. In a way, we can say that the world has been produced by substance out of a field of possibilities (But note that the evolutionary character of the world is only one in modal terms. In reality, noth-ing develops, because substance itself is already organized attributively such that everything is everywhere at the same time. This is the ancient definition of "eternity" (introduced by Boethius for example) which does not refer to infinite time (or space as to that), but to the *absence* of both. If a theory of evolutionary systems would like to be consistent within such an onto-epistemic picture, it identifies itself as an empirical theory of the human world (i.e., as one which is referring to processes which can be practically observed). Hence, it still needs a metaphysical (more general and intrinsically speculative) theory which serves as its foundation.). As seen under the modal perspective, worldly objects come into existence by some initial emergence of the world as we observe it which is thus an exteriorization of substance—in the sense that substance unfolds its or-ganizational structure. (This unfolding however is not really a dynamical process as we know it: Instead, it is rather an equivalent self-representation of substance itself. In other words: God calls his name, and the word becomes flesh.) So motion in terms of substance is essentially ill-defined. It is rather that substance is constituted as potentially self-moving in the sense that it is in a state of permanent self-fluctuation (or vibrational state) which represents an abstract, intrinsic sort of motion, a motion in-itself, of which the motion as we know it is a projection onto the human attributes which induce categories of space and time, respectively (Elsewhere this aspect has been discussed in view of a generalized concept of "freedom"; see Zimmermann, 1997a).

With respect to substance, the world as we observe it is in a kind of deficient state of substance as it appears only in terms of restrictions and constraints. Substance however, as foundation of the world as we observe it, is itself without foundation. Hence, it is entirely constituted in terms of self-reference, and in a sense, it propagates self-reference into the world as we observe it (Remember that the world as we observe it is only part of the world there is. In fact, because of the principle of immanence governing Spinoza's approach, there is no "beyond" of that world. What is *beyond our world* is simply the rest of the real world as it is defined in terms of the remaining infinity of attributes.). In principle then, the world can be eventually re-interiorized again, and it is this future state of worldly development (or evolution in fact) in which our historical existence can be reconciled again (or sublated in the threefold Hegelian sense) with the primordial unity of the real substantial totality. Whether this is a teleologically defined end of worldly evolution is however far from clear.

At this point, another clarifying remark should be in order: As we will be talking a lot about *evolutionary* systems in this present text, we should note that traditionally, the common terminology for this more recent version of systems theory is one which relies heavily on *worldly* aspects of (thus observable) processes. Hence, "evolution", as being defined in terms of some change of a system's state *in time* together with the meaning of being some sort of "unfolding" of some underlying potential of an initial "ground state" of that system, refers here to the "side of attributes" which is primarily subjected to the modelling performed by humans. In other words: As we deal here more with questions of a possible *foundation* of such systems rather than with practical applications within the domain of observable phenomena, we tend to treat time on the very same ontological footing as space. However, we are nevertheless still talking about evolutionary systems. The reason for this danger of conceptual ambiguity in the explicit meaning of space and time may be rooted in what we may call the "self-duality" associated with substance (an expression originating in quantum physics). I owe this important insight to a remark made by one of the book's referees.

CHAPTER 2

Spinozist Traces in the Theory of Evolutionary Systems

I t has not been before recently however (to be more precise: at the ISES 1995 meeting in Vienna) that evolutionary systems have been discussed in a larger circle of those who would like to base the theory of systems onto modern insight drawing on theories of self-organization (from the seventies of the 20th century referring to names such as Thom, Prigogine, Atlan, Morin and others) and chaos (including fractal geometries) as well as theories of complexity, emergence, and artificial life (from the eigthies and nineties, respectively, referring to names such as Bak, Kauffman, Crutchfield, and others) (In fact, this movement has converged lately to fundamental physics, e.g., quantum gravity, on the one hand, and to quantum information theory, on the other. In the physics domain, the relevant names are Penrose, Isham, Smolin, Baez, L. Kauffman.). When we take a somewhat synthetic viewpoint here, we try to integrate the results of recent research in this sense into our general framework as we have developed it in the introduction.

Clearly, the emphasis lies on the process of foundational research, but the result is a practical one after all, because in its inner core the theory of evolutionary systems is primarily based on the close connection between the conceptualization of evolution on the one hand and of action on the other. Hence, the whole effort of acquiring knowledge is solely undertaken in order to eventually achieve explicit means of developing guidelines for a reasonable ethics (Van de Vijver *et al.*, 1998. From the preface of the editors: "It is important to see that describing the interactive history of systems in terms of stability and evolvability … fundamentally rearranges any discussion on values, aims, and purposes, and on individuality and subjectivity", p. x). And this is what shapes the explicit design of social space up to the infosphere to be actually approached as this present work's concrete objective. Such an attitude falls in line with the long tradition in philosophy originating in the metaphysical approach of Spinoza's: In a sense therefore, Spinoza can be actually visualized as an early inventor of this modern conception which deals with evolutionary systems in the first place (Atlan, 1998: 215-231).

2.1 The Onto-Epistemic Methodology—Logic and Hermeneutic

In fact, if generalizing the conceptual approach to a meta-theory of cognitive foundations which is primarily based on insight from mathematical topology (cf. Zimmermann, 2007a), we have to discuss here the relevance of the cognitive representation of the (philosophical) *category of space* in terms of the consequences implied by (mathematical) topos theory: In this sense, it can be shown that a topos is a Lindenbaum-Tarski algebra for a logical theory whose models are the points of a space. We can also show what kind of epistemic conclusions can be drawn from this result with a view to model theory and by doing so establish important relationships among the concepts of social space, networks, systems and evolutionary games on the one hand and semiosis on the other. We can thus achieve a suitable reconciliation of both the onto-epistemic (top-down) approach of the Kassel group (Zimmermann, 2004, 2007) and the evolutionary (bottom-up) approach of the Salzburg group (Hofkirchner *et al.*, 2007, http://icts.sbg.ac.at/media/pdf/pdf1490.pdf), respectively, carrying us forward among other things to fundamental aspects of *a unified theory of sociocomplexity and information*. It has been shown elsewhere that this approach is indeed compatible with the above mentioned philosophical tradition deriving from the metaphysical theory of Spinoza's (see more details in Zimmermann, 2000, 2002).

Indeed, in his foreword to Marcello Barbieri's book (Barbieri, 2003) Michael Ghiselin points to the process of reconstructing a system from incomplete information as being one of the most prominent components of *epigenesis* which Barbieri visualizes as the property of a system to increase its own complexity (Barbieri, 2003: x). In fact, Barbieri takes this capacity as a defining property of life itself. And it is accompanied by the properties of attaining both organic memories and organic codes. In fact, as it turns out, this approach is not far from what the Santa Fe school has put forward in the view of defining evolution in terms of an intrinsic unfolding of complexity by systems which tend to optimize their field of possibilities (cf. Kauffman, 2000). This is where virtuality comes into play: Indeed, Kauffman actually introduces what he calls a "fourth law" of thermodynamics in order to couple evolution with the practical acquiring of complexity. (The formulation is essentially: Evolution is such that developmental steps from a given state take place in the adjacent possible of this state. The adjacent possible is the set of possible states of a system which have exactly one reaction step distance from that state. Hence, this certifies that the field of possibilities is always larger than the field of actualities, and that evolution is based on local interactions.) But in order to phrase concepts like "complexity" and "emergence" in a manner which is sufficiently invariant, it is necessary to develop a new approach by means of a language which is both formal enough so as to cover the logic nucleus of the processes involved (which have their roots in processes usually described within the sciences) and also hermeneutic in the sense that its syntax serves the purpose of illuminating its semantics (as it is usually described in philosophy). A useful and promising approach has been introduced recently by Neuman and Nave which will be discussed shortly. As it turns out, it is the *language of mathematical categories* that seems appropriate to cover the aforementioned tasks. As we have shown at another place, a topological view which generically relates to the modern theory of systems is equally promising when trying to phrase the problems involved here.

On the other hand, somewhat earlier, it is Walter Fontana—a Santa Fe protagonist himself—who has shown how to approach an explicit convergence of various theories when describing chemical and biological structures within the framework of what he calls *alchemy*: The idea is that chemical molecules can be visualized as symbolic representations of operators which act upon chemical substances (Fontana, 1991). Insofar there is a structural similarity between a "chemical calculus" and the programming language LISP. This similarity motivates Fontana's "alchemy": An operator $op = f$ is defined then by its action on relevant variables $x, y, ...$: $f(x, y, ...)$. The result is the action's evaluation at the location $(x, y, ...)$. This viewpoint implies a correspondence table which couples the operator action of molecules to logic:

Physical molecule	Symbolical representation of an operator
Molecule behavior	Action of the operator
Chemical reaction	Evaluation of a functional term
Chemical properties of binding	Algebraic properties of connectives
Location of the reaction	Proposition
Stable molecule	Cut-free proof of the proposition
Complementarity	Negation
Reaction	Proof with Cut between proposition and negation

We see easily how concepts of the logical calculi of propositions and predicates enter the picture without leaving the framework of chemical reactions. The operator notation can be reproduced straightforwardly by means of the language LISP, because there the standard form of a command is the expression $(op\ x\ y)$ where empty input is significant now. Operators can be defined then by the command (define (op name x) (op x y)). And the crucial power of LISP lies in the aspect of self-recursion which admits procedures that can call on themselves. Hence, the natural logic associated with LISP is the Lambda calculus (This calculus has been utilized recently by Louis Kauffman within the field of theoretical physics, associated with results taken from knot theory. This approach has already established a deep and direct relationship between the fundamental aspects of physics and biology in terms of DNA replication. This calculus has been utilized recently by Louis Kauffman within the field of theoretical physics, associated with results taken from knot theory. This approach has already established a deep and direct relationship between the fundamental aspects of physics and biology in terms of DNA replication. See for details e.g., Boi (2005b). Note however that at the same time these very molecular situations represent observable properties of concrete objects that humans can handle in their everyday life. In other words: *The concrete structure of observable nature shows up as a pragmatic materialization of a logical language model.* Hence, consistent research turns out to be the process of performing self-consistent conventions of logical language models. The actual world (in the cognitive sense) is isomorphic to the world of functions as expressed in terms of operators which are at their base nothing but propositions. Essentially, this constitutes some sort of constructive feedback loop which defines a calculus of objects. The concept of operators serves as the conceptual connection between the internal structure of an object and the actions by which this same object takes part in the construction of other objects. Hence, there is a *space of possible objects*, and the organization of this space shows up algebraically as a network of mutually mediated paths of production. And here lies the relationship to mathematical topology: This is so because observable forms of objects (shapes) in the usual space of perception have the quality of the *phenotypes* of biology. They are points in a space of shapes. Spaces of this latter type can be treated in terms of topology, because they admit consistent criteria of "nearness". In other words: *Evolution is determined chiefly by the accessibility of points in shape space.* Note that this is also true for a heterogeneous variety of percolation problems, and what percolates is always some form of information.

In a recent work of theirs, Neuman and Nave (preprint, 2007) can demonstrate the relevance of (mathematical) categories for cognitively generated concept formation giving concrete examples from child development. Insofar they follow the essential line of argument as given by the late Piaget (Piaget *et al.*, 1992. See in particular Henriques, 1992: 183-206, ch. 13. [Note that although Piaget has not actually contributed to this volume by means of a paper of his own, it is nevertheless straightforward to assume that the program of his co-workers actually coincides with his own views.]). The basic idea is to represent the concept construction by means of pushout and pullback diagrams known from category theory: Take A, B, C as individual cases of some concept D* which is represented by the sign D playing in turn the role of denoting the respective cases as their associated name (Neuman & Nave chose D* = Dog*, D = Dog, A = Chihuahua, B = German Sheperd, C = Dachshound). Then the *pushout* is defined by a commuting diagram of the following form:

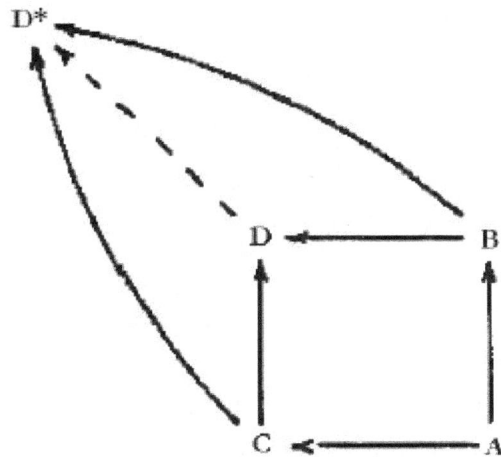

where upward pointing arrows indicate mappings to D*. In this sense, A is the *domain* of B and C which are in turn the *co-domains* of A. The mappings A ⇨ B and A ⇨ C are similarity indicators (identifiers) for the cases according to which case A can be consistently classified in order to associate it to a suitable underlying concept. Hence, this relation is a sort of equivalence relation. On the other hand, the mappings B ⇨ D and C ⇨ D associate the cases with names (they denote them). Then the *pushout* is given by the mapping u: D ⇨ D* which associates names with their appropriate concept such that the square diagram as part of the complete diagram commutes with u and the accompanying mappings of the upper left-hand cone. (The *pullback* then is the dual diagram which can be generated by simply reversing all directions of arrows.) The important point is that *only both diagrams together* can mediate case A with the concept D* in question such that it can be properly understood. In other words: The *pushout* refers to the conceptual reconstruction according to the *bottom-up method*, while the *pullback* refers instead to the conceptual reconstruction according to the *top-down method*. Hence, if both pushout and pullback do exist, we can formulate the result of a deductive algorithm: *If* case B is similar to case A *and if* case C is similar to A, *then* B is similar to C. We notice that the macrolevel (of concepts) and the microlevel (of individual cases) of reflexion determine each other in a mutual and circular manner. Hence, the syntactic as well as semantic dynamics of language reproduces the dynamics of self-organizing systems. Note that propositions of the type *if x ∪ if y, then z* conforms with lines of a computer program. In other words: The representation chosen here illustrates the close relationship between categories and the processing of information (computation) (see also Blass, 1988, preprint from the website. In this paper the author constructs the exact parallel by utilizing geometric morphisms which correspond to generalized continuous functions).

In fact, Neuman and Nave can show that this dual method of cognition covers equivalently the more complex case of *metaphorization* such that polysemy and degeneration of concepts add to strategic flexibility. Deduction is then replaced by *abductive inference*. We get a similar diagram as the one shown above:

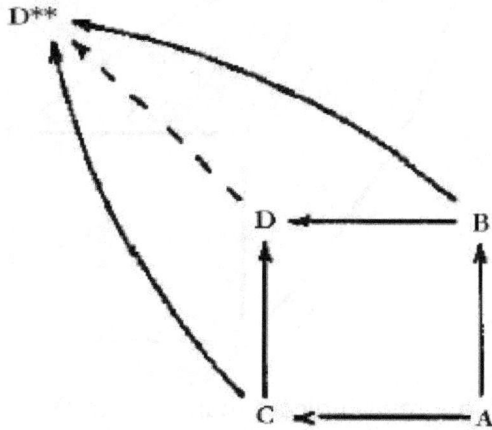

However, as the context is shifted now, metaphorization is a mapping of the type D* ⇨ D** such that commutation properties stay preserved (in the above example D could be used for Aunt Mary, say, who stands then for a person's quality D**). This is equally true, if in an even more complex case the name D is replaced by another D′ (In the mentioned example one can choose, e.g., D** such that D′ = Hot Dog). Then the diagram must be changed, if applying to the original concept in general:

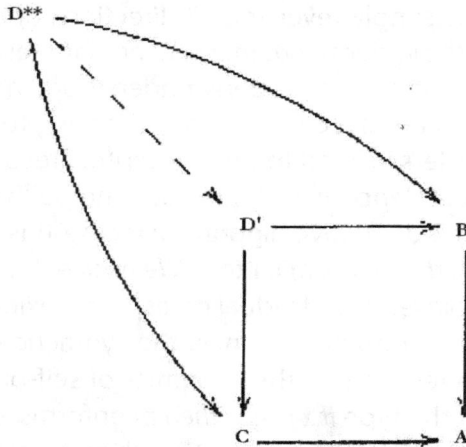

And instead of utilizing similarity mappings as identifyers and denotators ("is like" and "is a" as above), a negation shows up now ("is *not* like") in the diagram, if looking particularly at the mapping D′ ⇨ C (e.g., Dachshound *is like* a sausage, but a Chihuahua *is not like* the latter in the first case of metaphorizing our example. Or: Aunt Mary *is like* Aunt Ethel, but *is not like* a Chihuahua, respectively, in the second case). And note the reversal of the arrows directions. *Hence,*

the diagrams represent constraints which act onto the possible interpretations of signs. And the process of concept formation can thus create dynamical ontologies which are context-depending. Hence, we have a close relationship between semiosis by means of cognition and communication on the one hand, and logic on the other (This is what relates the foundations addressed here to the information concept of Luciano Floridi who has also coined the expression "infosphere". Cf. id. Information. In: Floridi, 2004).

We can generalize this promising approach by demonstrating in which sense pushout and pullback diagrams as introduced by Neuman and Nave into the semiological discussion of concept formation make it possible to define a *topos*. We follow here the presentations of the topic in various works of standard literature: See, e.g., Goldblatt (1984) and with respect to special perspectives chosen when introducing topoi: Bell (1988); Lambek & Scott (1986). Also very important: MacLane & Moerdijk (1992) and Johnstone (1977), and more recently Johnstone (2002, 2003). It is noteworthy to fix the terminology chosen by means of the general introduction of MacLane (1971), as well as with countless generalizing ideas by Freyd, Scedrov (1990). Among other, equivalent definitions, for us important here is the following definition which asserts that *a topos is a category with terminal object and pullbacks, with initial object and pushouts, with exponentials, and with a sub-object classifyer.* Note that the first two conditions are clearly demonstrated by using the diagrams introduced earlier. Case A of the respective name is an initial object of a category in the first version of the diagrams and a terminal object in the second version. So what we are talking about here is *a category of denotators* whose objects are the names of type D and whose morphisms are the identifyers (of two types: by denotating of the form "is a" and by comparing of the form "is like"). The various names of individual cases are sub-objects of the category. Mappings of the type $D \Rightarrow D^*$ and $D^* \Rightarrow D^{**}$, respectively, are functors between categories. Hence, we differ between the category of denotators and the category of concepts. And we differ between contexts such that the respective category of concepts is different from the one originally associated with the denotators. The first type of functor represents *deduction* (or *induction* as to that) while the second type represents *creative abduction*. In topos theory, a *subobject classifyer* is then essentially a generalized set of truth values Ω such that the diagram of the form:

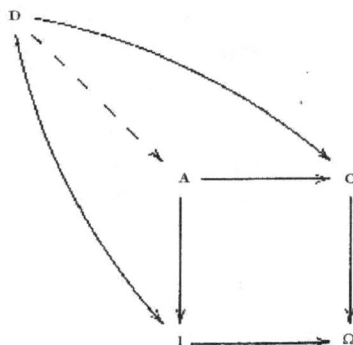

is a pullback. This time D is the denotator (name), A and C are two individual cases, and the mapping $1 \Rightarrow \Omega$ is a monic "true". (A *monic* is the categorial equivalent of a monomorphism which is an injective homomorphism.) The mapping $C \Rightarrow \Omega$ is called *characteristic arrow*. We can visualize what the subobject classifyer is actually doing by thinking of selecting those arrows which "come through" to the "truth" because they imply mutually compatible interpretations of names (This also clarifies the meaning of the subobjects themselves: Basically, a subobject of a C-object in a category C is thus a monic C-arrow with codomain in the target object. This is so because the domain of a monic is isomorphic to a subset of the codomain. And this also introduces *exponentials* which are simply all morphisms from a domain to a codomain of an object). Hence, we call the category of denotators utilized in the manner shown above *Neuman-Nave topos* (NN topos).

As already mentioned the important point is that a topos turns out to be a Lindenbaum-Tarski algebra for a logical theory whose models are the points of a space (we follow here the terminology of Vickers, 2002, preprint 2004). In other words, we can identify an appropriate space with a logical theory such that its points are the models of this theory, its open sets the propositional formulae, the sheafs the predicate formulae, and the continuous maps the transformations of models. At this point logic connects with model theory: Essentially, a Lindenbaum-Tarski algebra A of a logical theory T consists of the equivalence classes of propositions p of the theory under the relation $\cong$ defined by $p \cong q$ when p and q are logically equivalent in T. That is, in T proposition q can be deduced from p and vice-versa. Operations in A are inherited from those available in T, typically conjunction and disjunction. When negation is also present, then A is Boolean, provided the logic is classical. Conversely, for every Boolean algebra A, there is a theory T of classical propositional logic such that the Lindenbaum-Tarski algebra of T is isomorphic to A. In the case of intuitionistic logic, the Lindenbaum-Tarski algebras are Heyting algebras. (Hence, we deal here with an algebra of logical propositions in which logically equivalent formulations of the same proposition are not differentiated.) We recognize immediately that it is model theory which relates representation to interpretation. (And this is what the diagrams discussed above are all about.) In other words: *Model theory is the mathematical discipline that checks semantic elements of structures by means of syntactic elements in a given language.* The latter can have logical as well as non-logical symbols and grammatical rules, but in principle, it is always the explication of a logical theory. Is L such a language, and M some set, then M becomes an L-structure by means of the interpretation of each of the non-logical symbols in L. Each proposition which is formulated according to the rules gains some *meaning* in M. Hence, representation entails interpretation and vice versa.

It is not the proper place here to enter deeply into a discussion of model theory (for a useful survey refer to Hodges, 1997. See also in any case the famous works of Girard, 1989, 2003; Lawvere, 1963/1968). But what we can already notice is the relevance of the spatial approach to topoi: We recall from philosophical epistemology that essentially, a *theory* is a set of propositions which satisfy certain rules. If we visualize the theory as an abstract space, then the points of this space are subsets of propositions. Hence, generalized (abstract) spaces (not only within the field of mathematics) are nothing but sets of propositions or subsets of languages. Obviously, the languages serve the purpose of drafting out a picture of the world so as to orient oneself within its complex network of social and non-social interactions. Note that independent of the fact that we deal here with formal aspects of the theory, both logical as well as hermeneutical parts are being covered as to their consequences. (Note, e.g., that physical space as it is experienced in daily life is simply a projection of the more general though abstract social space onto its purely physical component. We come back to this later.)

This aspect can also be utilized when formally projecting processes onto a plane representing an abstract space of reflexive operations in the case of what we call *glass bead game* (cf. Zimmermann, 2005a. More details recently in Zimmermann, 2007b). The projection takes place here onto a two-dimensional plane which is represented in terms of vertices and edges of a network, where the vertices are points which represent propositions and the edges are logical connectives of these propositions. In principle, this is a graphical representation which illustrates nicely what the topos concept means when referring to its spatial aspect. The glass bead game consists of sequences of points being consistently connected by appropriate edges such that the resulting path within the network of propositions is the picture of a research process which mirrors the model building common in the sciences. (The idea is taken indeed from the well-known novel of Hermann Hesse's.) Hence, the glass bead game essentially maps a section of social space (namely its scientific section laid down in scientific scripture). And by doing so it also illustrates that this space is intrinsically dynamical, because it is actually constituted by the processing of the sequences of propositions according to given rules (syntax illuminating semantics). In other words: We deal here with *the processing of information* (including its organization and interpretation). This conception is well compatible with Lorenzer's theory of "language games" stressing the importance of predicators for the explicit training of social interactions in daily life (cf. Lorenzer, 1970, 1977. Originally, Lorenzer looked for a theoretical combination of Wittgenstein's and Freud's approaches).

One aspect is still missing which is the concrete *multi-perspectivity* of social space. This is in fact dealt with in detail in the work of Mazzola in order to take the various perspectives into account which determine the modes of interpretation of given works of music. But this aspect is equally important for social spaces in general. And as it turns out, it can also be included in the terminology of topos theory. This can be shown in terms of what is called "Yoneda lemma": For Mazzola, what the Yoneda lemma clarifies, is that it serves as a foundation of multi-perspectivity among local interpretations: In music, let R and S be appropriate vector spaces, and let K in R and L in S be two local compositions (We refer here to Mazzola, 1997. The complete outline of Mazzola's approach is given in the monumental book Mazzola, 2002). The relations then between the two compositions can be expressed as a morphism $K \Rightarrow L$. Essentially, this morphism defines a perspective under which L can be visualized. (In fact, we can construct similar pushout and pullback diagrams as shown in the case of the NN topos.) *The Yoneda lemma certifies then that the system of all L-perspectives determines the isomorphy class of L.* In other words: The morphisms can be visualized as essentially hermeneutic instruments in order to classify and understand local compositions. It is quite straightforward then to generalize this aspect to more "unspecialized" cases as instances of social space. The important point is that most of the time we do not talk here about a space *as it is actually observed*, but instead about a space *as it could be observed*. In other words: The number of possible interpretations is larger than the number of actual interpretations. (Remember that in common social space collections of these interpretations form the practical "world-view".) Hence, not only shows space up as social space in the first place, and not only shows social space up as a space whose points are propositions of logical theories, but moreover social space shows up as well as a *virtual space*. Strictly speaking then, social space is a *special case* of virtual space, and not vice versa, because the latter's "virtuality" refers to the field of possibilities rather than to the field of actualities which can be empirically observed. Hence, topos theory can also be visualized as a kind of "calculus of possibilities". This is what relates this present approach directly to the conceptions of existential philosophies as exemplified in the models presented equally by Jean-Paul Sartre as well as Ernst Bloch (Zimmermann, 2002b/2001a and http://arxiv.org/ ftp/physics/papers/0105/0105094.pdf. Also in: Science & Society, Polish Academy of Sciences, Scientific Centre, Paris, 2002: 17-32).

What we see now is that traditionally, there have been already many connections between the human techniques of spatial representation (what has been called *anthropological graphism* elsewhere (Zimmermann, 2004a. The idea goes back to a formulation of Henri Lefebvre: The Production of Space, Blackwell, Oxford, 1991 (1974): 33. "A conceptual triad has now emerged ...: 1) *spatial practice* which embraces production and reproduction, and the particular locations and spatial sets characteristic of each social formation… 2) *representations of space* which are tied to the relations of production…, hence to knowledge, signs, codes… 3) *representational spaces* embodying complex symbolisms … linked to the clandestine side of social life…" Note that in this book the problem of space is posed for the first time in a sufficiently modern language. There are even some remarks on Hesse's glass bead game (Lefebvre, 1991/1974: 24, 136)) and the mapping of processes in terms of logical formulae. The approach of Fontana is one example, very much on the line of the Santa Fe school on self-organized criticality. We have also seen that this kind of discussion visualizes processes in the general sense as percolation phenomena (cf. Stauffer, Aharony, 1994), and what is being percolated is information then. And we have seen that it is topos theory that provides an appropriate language in order to deal with these aspects of spatial representation. More than that: A topos can be essentially interpreted as the algebraic expression of the fact that spaces utilized in human cognition are basically constituted by propositions of logical theories. On the other hand, the procedures of deduction and induction as well as creative abduction, available to human logic, can be rephrased in terms of algorithmic procedures. Hence, they are both accessible by means of programmes as they are utilized in computation, and by means of game theory, because on a fundamental level of reflexion games are essentially algorithmic procedures whose strategies are given by its rules (cf. Houston, 2003).

What we realize then is that all of this relates nicely to the approaches of the Kassel and Salzburg schools as described at earlier occasions (cf. the volumes of collected essays presenting the results of the INTAS cooperation project "Human Systems in Transition" with the universities of Vienna, Kassel, Kyiv, and the Academy of Sciences, Moscow led by Hofkirchner (then Vienna, now Salzburg), namely by Arshinov & Fuchs, 2003). Also Dobronravova & Hofkirchner, 2004; Zimmermann & Budanov, 2005). And we gain a consistent representation of what we can call "logic of design" laying the grounds for designing social space(s) explicitly by means of modeling them in the first Note that the conceptual nucleus of these approaches is given by the two triadic arrangements of concepts of form which are fundamental for both the approaches of the Salzburg as well as Kassel groups:

Cognition	Communication	Cooperation
Space	Network	System

The first triadic structure mirrors the close relationship between cognition and communication on the one hand—as pair of concepts characterizing the process of reflexion—and cooperation on the other hand—as characterizing the transition from reflexion to action (see for more details Zimmermann, 2008a). While the first pair of concepts cannot be separated in practise, the latter concept is structurally separable from the other two. Reflexion and action represent thus two different time scales which show up together with the systematic updating process involved in the sequential organization which is underlying both reflexion and action, respectively. The producing of models belongs to this pair of concepts in the first place and is primarily based on a generic self-model which defines the framework according to which cognition is normalized. Essentially, this is the onto-epistemic picture of the grasping of the world by humans (In other words: It is the human mode of being to produce knowledge. Hence, for humans, ontology and epistemology fall into one. Higher and lower animals, in principle also plants, represent the same scheme, but on lower levels of organization. Essentially, even physical systems on a very fundamental level can be thought of as satisfying the general framework of this scheme, though by extremely simple means of organization. In the sense of Stuart Kauffman, the most fundamental physical (autonomous) agent can be defined by satisfying a minimal condition from thermodynamics: namely that the system is able to perform at least one thermodynamic work cycle. This is probably true for spin networks on the level of quantized physical space. Hence, evolution shows up as a multi-shifted hierarchy of complexity as to the unfolding of various forms of organized collectives of (autonomous) agents. Humans represent thus systems with (up to now) maximal degree of organization. In between we would expect a manifold of biological structures with different degrees of organization smaller than that degree in humans). Earlier stages of evolution can be visualized as conceptual approximations of this onto-epistemic picture. In *methodological* terms the second triadic structure is associated with the first such that there are intrinsic pairwise correspondences between cognition and space, communication and network, and cooperation and system, respectively. In other words: *Space is the conceptual structure from which that world of daily life is being reconstructed which is derived from the process of cognition. Network is the conceptual structure from which those social interactions of daily life can be reconstructed which are derived from the process of communication. System is the conceptual structure from which those joint manipulations of the material world can be reconstructed which are derived from the process of cooperation.* Obviously, the first and second pair of concepts from the two triadic structures regulate the actual flow of information and the interpretation of meaning while the third pair regulates the production of matter. This is a result of the fact that the complete system is more than space and network, because it does not only encompass social interactions, but also tangible matter (of course, these two make no difference with respect to both the energy balance and the entropy balance. Matter belongs to the additional term which has to be added on the entropy's side in order to make both balances equal, because it can be visualized as a kind of stored information (memory)). In a sense, space is the region in which the system unfolds its actions, while the network is skeleton/circulation/backbone of both space and system. Hence, we can clearly show here how humans construct their various spatial representations by means of editing the propositions of their theories.

Due to the properties of topos theory we can rewrite algebraic expressions as logic expressions such that diagrams commute, e.g., for the case of negation we have:

$$1 \xrightarrow{\text{false}} 2$$
$$\downarrow \qquad \downarrow \neg$$
$$1 \xrightarrow{\text{true}} 2$$

When passing over from Boolean to intuitionistic logic, then we have to take into account that the former is governed by Boolean algebras and the latter by Heyting algebras. The important difference between these two is in the negation operation. In the Boolean case negation shows up as "complementarization", similar to the case of duality: $\neg(\neg x) = x$. In other words: The negation of the negation reproduces the proposition again. In the case of a Heyting algebra however, this is not true anymore. Instead, we have now: $\neg(\neg x) \neq x$. This means in particular that recursive operations make the emergence of innovative structures possible. Categories become time-dependent, contrary to sets, because objects can be created as well as annihilated. (Already in the calculus of propositions can we find the consequences of this formal difference between the types of algebra. We have discussed the more elementary aspects of logic, especially with a view to the classical form of propositional calculus, e.g., with respect to the *modus ponens* elsewhere. See, e.g., in Loh *et al.*, 2008, (in print) part 3. We find that if f: $A \rightarrow B$ is a morphism in the topos C, then the functor $\text{Sub}(B) \rightarrow \text{Sub}(A)$ of Heyting algebras has a right-adjoint ∀ as well as a left-adjoint ∃. (Obviously, Heyting algebras and thus intuitionistic logic is more generic for topos theory than Boolean classical logic.)

There is an interesting hermeneutic side-aspect to all of this: In the Lacanian terminology of negations the classical Aristotelian logic is being generalized in terms of a philosophical rather than mathematical discourse. For the classical tradition there is a total (absolute) truth pointing to the complete conformity of language and being which transcends the merely partial truth implied by the analytic discourse. For Aristotle, universality implies existence (Juranville, 1990: 397). For Lacan however there is an implicit "schismogenesis" of writing and talking such that a generalization is necessary which takes this difference into account. For him, this results in an extension of the negation operations as indicated by the following schematic table:

$$\forall x.\, f(x) \qquad \exists x.\, f(\neg x)$$

$\forall x.\, f(x)$	$\exists x.\, f(\neg x)$
$\forall x.\, f(\neg x)$	$\exists x.\, f(x)$
$\neg\forall x.\, f(x)$	$\neg\exists x.\, \neg f(x)$

Nothing comes to its determination except by means of difference (as Spinoza already knew), and the universal is not the universal of an essence. In fact, the potential of denotation is questioned in the process of signification. Lacan's *ré-écriture* constitutes thus a new sort of scripture which represents/misrepresents the limits of the scripture of science. In a sense, Lacan generalizes the idea of Goedel's by pointing to a beyond of scientific scripture. Hence, he introduces two qualified negations which replace the classical negation and add two new propositional forms to the table above: $\neg\forall$: discordant negation (denying/disclaiming negation) vs. $\neg\exists$: rejecting negation. Therefore, the field of science's scripture is the world, but the truth of significants cannot be formulated under the form of knowledge. Knowledge means to signify what is part of the world. The sort of knowledge therefore which is expressed within the psycho-analytic discourse is instead of the type of the *mathema* which is the generalized form of the table above. For us here, this aspect is important with a view to the recent enterprises in theoretical physics as well as in music theory (and somewhere in between) to actually introduce a formal language which is capable of achieving a unified discourse with a logical nucleus and a hermeneutic halo for both syntax and semantics. (We refer here to the cases mentioned earlier of ongoing research by Christopher Isham *et al.* on the one hand and Guerino Mazzola *et al.* on the other.)

2.2 Conclusion—The Ethics of Evolutionary Systems

Not until recently has the research on ethical consequences of evolutionary theories gained a certain amount of minimal attention after a long while of sole reference to Gerhard Vollmer's approach (cf.e.g., in K. Bayertz (ed.), 1993. Also Vollmer, 1975/1998. A recent debate can be found in EWE (Deliberation, Knowledge, Ethics) 18/3, 2007: 443-480 with a view to an essay of Ernst R. Sandvoss. See in particular Zimmermann, 2007c: 476-478.). If we refer back to the Spinozist conception again—in order to observe the conceptual consistency of the afore-mentioned traditional line of argument—we find that the crucial task of this sort of ethics (the examination and verification of adequacy) is straightforwardly based on the acquiring of knowledge about the essential conditions put forward in the theory of evolutionary systems. If the result is indeed that the propositional structure of theories (both logical, i.e., scientific, and pre-scientific) determines the inherent spatiality of human thinking and the concrete shape of communicative networks, then obviously, the question is how to actually modify this very propositional structure (or in other words: the governing discourse) of social systems in order to achieve an improvement of the living conditions. Hence, it is the progressive shaping of communication which is in the centre of the main tasks of ethical theory: If it turns out that the observed actions are inadequate, then it is the objective of ethics to give hints as to the possible changing of the framework of the conditions of these actions such that inadequate actions as their consequences are not anymore necessary.

This is indeed what ethics has to offer to politics and general law. But ethics also continues in order to explicate these results to those who were committed to inadequate actions in the first place. In his "socialist ethics" Sartre has given illuminating examples for this point.

Hence, *from where we started* were indeed the results as offered by modern interpretations of the consequences as derived from the substance metaphysics of Spinoza's, by the recent research on artificial life and self-organized criticality as pursued by the Santa Fe school, and by the conception of mathematical topos theory mainly achieved by Lawvere, MacLane, Johnstone and others. *What we ourselves have achieved so far then* has been the conceptual foundation of the two significant triads displayed above: on the one hand by analyzing the consequences of the role of structural self-organization as independent regulator and framework generator of other processes in evolutionary systems such as selection and mutation (as was done within the joint INTAS project during the years 2000 through 2005), on the other hand by establishing a methodological bridge between philosophical hermeneutic and logic and the presently convergent sciences involved such as physics, biology, and computer science, respectively, by means of introducing a mathematically grounded conceptualization of the scientific language as originating in topos theory, locating here the roots of the deep interrelationship between logic and cognition (as was done during the years 2005 through 2007 in the Kassel group in close cooperation with the Salzburg group). *What we would like to achieve* is a theoretical architecture which clearly displays in some detail the systematic interactions by which the observed phenomena with respect to the two triads of concepts are being steered. Besides establishing a new cognitive meta-theory very much on the line of Freud's psychoanalysis, modern biosemiotics, or design science, this also results in explicit practical strategies in the empirical field. And this is what ethics shall actually achieve: to clarify adequacy of behavior, to tell how to modify its pre-conditions provided the result shows inadequacy, and to tell what should happen with those who acted inadequate in the first place—very much in the sense as laid down by Spinoza some 350 years ago. *The method by which we try to achieve this objective* is the consequent analyzing of the concrete mediation of cognition and communication in terms of recent methods both from the hermeneutic and logic inventory of classical philosophy as well as from the formal inventory of mathematics and the sciences.

CHAPTER 3

The First Conceptual Triad (Concerning the Nature and Origin of the Mind I)

In order to clarify our viewpoint with respect to the individual components of what we have called the first conceptual triad, we start from the concept of socialization: We have already seen that the first two components of the triad, of the form

Cognition	Communication	Co-operation

are coupled to each other more closely than to the third, because, in principle, the constitutive period of cognition cannot be separated from the active influence of ongoing communication—long before explicit cooperation becomes relevant in practical terms. At the same time, socialization illustrates clearly the need for the already mentioned *cognitive metatheory* of theories which takes this original mediation of cognition and communication into account, once we agree to visualizing theories themselves as representation of what is actually being thought of.

We can find one possible starting point for these ideas in two perspectives taken with respect to the underlying ontology and epistemology of approach: *On the one hand*, we talk about the validity of the "principle of emergence" related to the recent theories of evolutionary systems. The main point of this principle is simply *that the world is not such as humans perceive it* (This main point we have discussed at various other places, e.g., in Zimmermann (ed.), 2006, cf. also Zimmermann, 2007a). Hence, for all phenomena in the world, there is an *essentially unobservable microlevel* on which the processes happen in *real* terms and an *observable macrolevel* on which phenomena are being perceived in *modal* terms. Obviously, phenomena can be understood sufficiently, if it is possible to re-construct the microlevel according to the observations made on the macrolevel.

This was demonstrated by means of describing the foundations for re-constructing the historical centre of the city of Bologna (cf. Zimmermann *et al.*, 2001 Part I: Basic Idea & Fundamental Concepts, http://arxiv.org/ftp/nlin/papers/0109/0109025.pdf). On the macrolevel all that is being observed what determines the experience of urban space such as the architecture, the traffic flow, the economic functions and so forth. These are phenomena which determine the city as city and are equally accessible to all the by-passers who can thus describe them in turn. On the microlevel however all those processes take place which cause the observable phenomena in the first place: The installation of a building, e.g., is a complex mixture of multiple, coupled micro-processes which cannot all be observed in detail. Hence, the former is *emergent* with respect to the latter. Obviously, the one has to be described in a language which is different from the language chosen in order to describe the other. In fact, a straightforward method in order to localize the respective level of consideration is to check whether the languages utilized possess concepts which are mutually irreducible or not. We deal here a lot with mathematics when discussing possibilities to reconstruct the microlevel according to observations made on the macrolevel. We thus illuminate the derivative mediation of the methodology with the methods of physics and logic, respectively. But we also recognize how much it is the *hermeneutic of nature* that is in question here: Instead of the methods of deduction and induction which have come upon us, we have to deal then with what Umberto Eco once called *creative abduction*.

On the other hand, we still note the following important point: The hierarchical derivative structure of the various disciplines involved implies in so far a degree of *interdisciplinarity*, where we have to differ carefully between what the actual model chosen expresses in concrete terms, and what is chosen as representation of this model. In other words, we always talk about *representations of representations* or *models of models* rather than about what is really there after all and what could be described in some sense of absolute truth. To understand this is necessary for avoiding to look for the onto-epistemic difference where there is none, and it deals with all the possible disciplines, philosophy included, on the very same footing.

Hence, we can clearly recognize that in principle, we deal with communication all the time: Because representation of models does not suffice in order to grasp a problem, if it is not *presented* at the same time, i.e., offered to the ongoing debate within the public discourse. Research means thus communication of insight in the first place. In this sense, research on space is *topology of communication* rather than mere topology. (This has a double connotation as to including the mathematical field of describing space as well as the field of the humanities dealing with linguistic topoi. Moreover, this is the reason for staying with the plural "topoi" for the mentioned mathematical structure (as generalized category) contrary to the etymologically uncorrect but widely spread use of "toposes". Hence, we follow here the choice made by Goldblatt.)

Visualized this way, such a topology gains also the connotation of founding a desired "metapsychology" which might be able to provoke a general science of design: Although this aspect goes back to Freud, it is nevertheless implied by basic insight provided by Spinoza who—as we have seen before—differs between what he calls reality and modality. But by doing so he also avoids any reference to idealistic transcendence: Instead, he replaces it by *materialistic immanence* assuming a world which is one totality that can only be grasped partially by humans according to their two available attributes such that the identity theorem is valid.

In the case of Freud now the cognitive aspect comes more and more into focus: It is under the impression of reading Taine's book (Taine, 1880, 1870) that Freud develops the conception of *metapsychology* (Letter to Fliess of 13. 2. 1896: "Psychology—*meta*psychology to tell the truth—is with what I am permanently dealing, the book of *Taine* "L'Intelligence" fits my purposes extraordinarily well." Freud, 1986: 181—our own translation) the sources of which will remain however rare. In the 1915 text called "The Unconscious" Freud writes:"I propose that we shall speak of a *metapsychological* representation, if we are successful in describing a psychic process according to its *dynamical, topical and economic* relations." (Freud, 1982, volume 3: 140). This formulation is especially interesting for us today, because the collection of the attributes chosen here connote modern problems, even if we have to modify the terminology somehow. This is mainly so, because we have indeed to deal with a methodological recombination of dynamics, topics, and economics, respectively, as we have already seen above in more detail. It is Patricia Kitcher who visualizes thus Freud as the "first interdisciplinary scientist of cognition" (Kitcher, 1992: 5). In Freud's project she recognizes a continuation of the traditional hierarchization of the sciences which started with Auguste Comte and without which it would not be possible to understand Freud's main work (the *Interpretation of Dreams*) at all (Kitcher, 1992: 6sq.). In fact, she moreover does not recognize a crucial contradiction in the fact that the sciences of the 19th century were primarily conceptualized as evolutionary, while the cognitive sciences of today are primarily conceptualized as computational (Kitcher, 1992: 8. In German, contrary to English and French, this concept is difficult to express without encountering some phonetic dissonance. But in general, it is clearly established now in the theories of systems. "Computation" does not only connote the calculating of procedures, but also, and more so, the systematic ordering and the logical combining, deducing, abducing and so forth. In principle, also the computer is an instrument which deals with the *reprocessing of information* rather than with calculating. This is particularly obvious in the case of cellular automata which have become important for the discussion of evolutionary processes. See the important Wolfram, 2002).

Hence, we have to take into account that each theory to be developed has to be referred to what we can call *the human nature of knowledge*. In other words: *For each theory there is a cognitive metatheory*. Probably, Freud visualized the nucleus of psychoanalysis as such a metatheory. In principle, we can also visualize the political economics of Marx as belonging to this sort of theory. Obviously, independent of the success these approaches did actually have, they have in common a general intention of starting from human constitution in terms of cognition, communication, and cooperation, respectively. In a sense, this is something which binds them in conceptual terms to the various approaches of the theory of evolutionary systems as provided by Bertalanffy and several others.

With a view to Bloch we realize that the concept of "harmony" introduced there (i.e., *succeeding reconciliation*) points to a similar metatheoretical perspective. In particular, the specific criteria for this harmony depend on the concrete properties of theoretical representation. Indeed, at the same time, the underlying radical interdisciplinarity implies a polycontexturality of technical concepts which can be considered, if not as synonyms, but within a number of connotative equivalence relations. Most of all, this is the case for the concepts *space, network, system*. The frame of these relations can be illustrated by means of the following diagram:

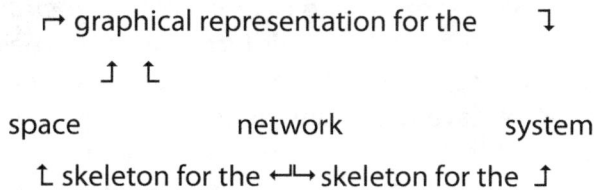

↦ graphical representation for the   ⌐

⌐ ⌐

space   network   system

⌐ skeleton for the ↤⊔↦ skeleton for the ⌐

As we have mentioned earlier, the key concept is "network" here which is the skeleton, circulation and/or backbone of space at the same time, spanned by the interactions which are in question. Hence, the network is a dynamical sort of skeleton which is the reason for the connotation of an organic circulation (of communicating information that is). On the other hand, the network is a similar skeleton for the system which is actually constituted by the given interactions. The system is thus the concrete correlate of representation. It is all what there is to a totality including that which is not communication. The space of the system is that region which is immanent to the action of its corresponding dynamical skeleton/circulation/backbone. That is, within it, the explicit loci of active possibilities unfold. The interactions among these loci which are operators and components of the system at the same time, are represented as force lines in the network originating at the network's knots, the vertices (This is the practical relevance of mathematical formalization: Independent of the nature of the processes in question, it is possible to qualify the interactions among knots in terms of codifiable numbers which show up as components of the matrix representation of that group actions which originate from the knots visualized as operators.). Hence, in this sense, the topology here is a theory of networks and a theory of (evolutionary) systems at the same time.

It is this viewpoint which determines the onto-epistemic orientation of further work: Presently, there are mainly two kinds of practical ignorance which make it difficult to find orientation. On the one hand we have what we may call the illiteracy of *visual cognition*. On the other hand we have the illiteracy of *formal conceptualization*. In particular, both these forms of ignorance diminish the capabilities of spatially grasping the environment quite decisively. However, it is only the understanding of the boundary conditions that are prescribed by the structure of experiencable space, and of the rich repertoire of possible forms of behavior within the framework of these boundary conditions that is necessary in order to explicate adequate behavior in professional as well as private everyday life. Hence, it is only this sort of insight in the mediative action of the organized space that makes *ethics* possible (cf. Loeb, 1993). Similar to a grammar of music which consists of harmony, counterpoint and form, necessary to describe the structure of a composition, spatial structures, whether organized in an architectural or choreographic way, do possess their grammar which consists of parameters such as symmetry, proportion, connectivity, valence, and stability. Space is thus no passive vacuum. Instead it possesses active properties which restrict or enhance the structures by which it is inhabited. It is *design science* which deals with the discussion of such grammars in detail (Loeb, 1993:1 (par.)). The concept of harmony already mentioned here points first of all to the complex manifold of geometrical forms. In principle, one may call such an approach to space *formal harmonics* which denotes a field of research that combines methods of topology, geometry, and physics, but also methods which are dealing with hermeneutic aspects. Hence, there are "two dimensions" which lead forward into this *interdiscipline* and open up at the same time a historical perspective. So on the one hand, there are fields of mathematical modeling, on the other, there are regions of creative design. Both these fields can be visualized as different components of one and the same *design science* which tries to incorporate them in practical terms (cf. Kappraff, 2001). These two components act in unison within the everyday medium of practical behavior. And there are systems in which everything interacts in a complex environment: systems of urban space (cf. Winkler, 1998).

Its universality design science gains by the unified conception as to the strategic beginning of a modeling process: We begin with a general arrangement of observable structures to patterns (taxonomies) and the development of associative contexts mediating superstructures among them. It follows the straightforward definition of a suitable system and its underlying structures and substructures (by means of localizing its boundary). This illustrates the mentioned analogy with language in general: There is a given lexicology, a syntax, and a semantic of the explicit modeling language. *Hence, there are possibilities of systems design*. In other words: what we mean with *design* is to emulate a system in practical terms and to define the transformation of the results into strategic applications. *Hence, design science constructs epistemic strategies out of the universal mediation of cognition and modeling*. Consequently, the field of applications of this approach is not restricted in any respect. In this sense, design science gains its connotation of being a suitable *cognitive metatheory* for (all) other theories.

In fact, the mentioned principles of harmony come into play then by noting the necessity of checking the manifold of subsystems as to their symmetry properties and other harmonical criteria. *Hence, design science means transformation of information.* And the accumulation of relevant knowledge and the latter's management are the first step towards this process. In other words: *Design science is the science of organizing and transforming relevant information* (http://deed.megan.ryerson.ca/DesignScience/, M. Ryerson: *Design Science and its Goals*). Visualized this way, we recognize that in this sense, a future topology of communication may serve as the nucleus of a future design science.

CHAPTER 4

The Second Conceptual Triad (Concerning The Nature And Origin Of The Mind II)

In order to suitably situate the second triad now, of the more methodological structure of the kind:

Space	Network	System

we may start with the concept of "hodological space", thus beginning with the "cognitive side" of the discussion.

In his first main work (Being and Nothingness, Sartre, 1943, Quoted here according to the German edition of 1993), Sartre introduces the concept of *hodological space* choosing the example of Proust's novel (On Search for Time Lost) when declaring: "[…] being is *situated*, not by means of its relative position to the locations, not by means of degrees of longitude and latitude, respectively: It situates itself within a human space, between the 'world of the Guermantes' and the 'world of Swann'. And it is the immediate presence of Swann, of the duchess of Guermantes, which makes it possible to unfold this 'hodological space', exactly where it situates itself" (Sartre, 1943: 500sq, here and in the future always our own translation).

Sartre centres his discussion around to basic aspects: On the one hand, we talk here about a space which is *charged with meaning* such that it differs from the formally given physical space as well as from geographical space which serves the mere cartographization of locations. And this meaning is being extracted from social connotations of concrete "areas of presence" which are being associated in turn with concrete persons. On the other hand, these persons are *concrete* in the sense that they do not only exist in an actual manner (or have existed), but they are capable of unfolding practical actions by means of their *cognitive presence*. If for instance, the protagonist of the novel is used to perform the famous Sunday walks, once towards the "side" of the Guermantes, at other times towards the "side" of Swann, then this geographical ritual evokes a connotative characterization of a walking path which is in itself nothing but a geographical property of a route, present even, if the mentioned persons do never show up. (Little Marcel who performs these walks together with his parents, does not know Swann nor the Guermantes, and he does not know anything about life style and social state, but the discourse of the grown ups *about* Swann and the Guermantes formatizes the pattern of associations connected with this walking path and excites the imagination: Hence, it is not the actual meeting of these persons which irrealize them within imagination, but it is this imagination which prescribes the first meeting in the future, in the first place.) Sartre notes that the presence of those persons takes place "in transcendence": "…the transcendent presence of my cousin from Morocco permits me to unfold between himself and myself this route which situates myself within this world and which one could call the way to Morocco" (Sartre, 1943: 501). This is what happens to children when experiencing their first environment: There are names which catalyze the emergence of imaginative pictures which in turn are closely connected from then on to locations and paths between locations and saved once and for all in their memory such that later these pictures can be recalled within the framework of other contexts or at other occasions. Indeed, they *have* already produced some *basic attitude* that defines the relationship between a person's mentality with respect to these locations and paths. It is this sense in which socialization is actually being structured. (Compare this with what we said about names in the context of mathematical topoi!)

This is what Ernst Bloch means with his intuitive concept of *home* which emerges within these first impressions in the run of early socialization: „Have the humans grasped themselves then, and founded theirs without any exteriorization and alienation within real democracy, there emerges something in the world which shines all of them into their childhood and in which nobody has been yet: home." (Bloch, 1982 (1959), volume 3: 1628, our own somewhat adapted translation).

Note that these first impressions of the first hodological space experienced *do not yet constitute* home in an explicit sense, but instead they draft out what in the future home could actually be. In other words, it is necessary to extract the *general qualities* which are the fundamental elements of a *common* space of communication (actually of a space of free play essentially produced by means of communication). In the words of Bloch: "I am. But I do not have myself yet. Thus we are still becoming" (Bloch, 1985: 1 (13. Tuebinger Einleitung in die Philosophie. Suhrkamp, Frankfurt a. M., 1985, 13). With a view to possible interpretations of this formulation see Zimmermann, 1997b). Hence, a home emptied of concrete persons is no home, but a region of origin at most which can unfold those connotations at best which imply symbolical orientations of the individual biography. But only the concrete persons can approximate what Bloch calls home, namely in designing the communicative discourse. Nothing else means Sartre: "Hence, I am *situated* by the infinite variety of those paths which conduct myself to objects of *my* world, in correlation to the immediate presence of transcendental subjects" (Sartre, 1943: 501) (Note that it is thus necessary that the persons in question are concretely available or have been available, but just now they have not necessarily to stand in front of myself. In this sense, they are transcendent, but nevertheless present. They are, in order to paraphrase a well-known example which Sartre utilizes from time to time, *a present absence*, like the famous Pierre with whom I have an appointment in a café, but who has not yet shown up and who perhaps is not coming at all (Sartre, 1943: 59sqq.). In Sartre the concept of present absence prepares the even more prominent concept of the *look*: "… in each look there is the appearance of some object-other as concrete and probable presence in my field of perception … This 'being looked at' offers itself as pure probability for my presently being this concrete *that*— a probability which can gain its meaning and just its probability only out of a fundamental certainty that the other is always present for me in so far as I am always *for others*" (Sartre, 1943: 503). In this early work of Sartre's the conception is primarily oriented in terms of two aspects: the phenomenological aspect in the sense of Husserl's philosophy, and the ontological determination of the human mode of being. Hence, to be for others is in Sartre the characteristic mode of being for humans which expresses itself in phenomenological terms as lived experience amidst the others. In other words: The hodological space is the ontologically relevant representation of this mode of being and thus its explicit epistemological comprehension. Hence, the ontological space is always constituted itself as *onto-epistemic*. Obviously, this space can hardly be thought of as anything else than a space which is *publicly* structured. Therefore, it is also—even as the first hodological space of early childhood—the stage on which a person is going to enact him/herself. In this sense, the communicative discourse is always produced as one which is strategically constituted in the first place, because from the beginning on a strategy is intrinsic to the aforementioned enactment.

There is an example discussed in detail by Sartre himself which is suitable for illustrating the above mentioned aspects: This is the episode of a strategically proposed Punch and Judy show organized by little Sartre in the Jardin du Luxembourg. We have discussed this episode several times in other places, and we will not elaborate on it here (cf. Zimmermann, 2002a (2nd edition 2004): 55sqq. —Sartre tells this episode in his diary entry of 28th Februar 1940 in Sartre, 1984: 382sqq. (= Les carnets de la drôle de guerre, Gallimard, Paris, 1983: 320sqq.). For us here important is however to understand that this episode would be quite unimportant, if the hodological space of Sartre (that is the southern environment of the Quartier Latin in Paris) would not be actually filled with discourses which can be visualized as practical interpretations of their own significations: Only, *because* Sartre lets his personal interpretations become practical, the hodological space proves itself as being connoted. And in this sense, it is already constituted in a strategical way. The concrete persons therefore to whom the hodological space is implicitly referring all the time, mutually produce those discursive dispositions which act upon the others who are also part of the same space such that adequate discourse-dominating strategies offer themselves *as if by their own activity*. Hence, for Sartre, humans are constituted in a relational sense: "To appear is for me to unfold my distances with respect to the objects, and by doing so make objects appear" (Sartre, 1932: 547). The world answers to my being there, and I answer to the being there of the world. In this sense, my knowledge is always *engaged* knowledge: "That is, knowledge and acting are only two abstract sides of an original and concrete relationship. The real space of the world is the space Lewin calls 'hodological'" (Sartre, 1932).

Originally, this expression goes back to the Berlin gestalt psychologists, especially to Kurt Lewin who introduces the term for the first time in a paper published in 1934 (Lewin, 1934. This approach is discussed in more detail in: Lewin, 1936). In particular, Lewin refers here to the paths which structure the immediate environment of a person by means of a network (Hence, the expression from the Greek word *hólos*, the path/route.). Physiologically, the cognitive scanning of this environment is being saved by means of "cognitive maps" which themselves are structured in terms of networks. In other words—we will discuss this later in more detail—human perception shows up as one which is fitted to network representations in the first place. The relevant *loci* thus constitute space by arranging landmarks, paths, nodes, districts, and edges in an explicit network setting (Frohnhofen, 2001: 32). The memorizability of *loci* is important for the associative organization of space which depends primarily on *marks of good form*. The explicit criteria for coded representations in turn depend on the connotative charges in the sense described above: The mediated intensity of a location is being determined by the lived connotative relevance of the persons that span hodological space (Frohnhofen, 2001: 34). Although in the beginning space is perceived this way as a container or stage in (on) which social enactment actually takes place, the network itself generates at once individual meaning producing aspects such that the location within the network gains its own *genius loci* (Frohnhofen, 2001: 15sqq.). Achim Frohnhofen criticizes the absence of a modern theory of space (Frohnhofen, 2001: 12), but in principle, he follows the model of gestalt psychology. Indeed, this present text presents a new attempt to actually develop such a desired theory following the fundamental traces laid out by Spinoza.

We have already seen that space can thus be essentially visualized as a *cognitive principle of depth construction*: It secures the invariance of quantity and quality of perceived objects. Obviously, the significance of depth can be determined from physiological properties of the human organism, because the binocularity and the distance between the eyes imply spatial perception in the first place. While the adjustment of optical proximity and remoteness admits the fine tuning of manifold optical properties such as to allow orientation and manipulation accordingly. In particular, the composition of coverings, overlapping (implying the necessity of implicit completion), shadows, brightness, unfocusing (again, together with the proportionality of object size and object proximity, indicator of proximity and remoteness, i.e., depth), textual densities (gradient criteria which are thus direction-orienting), dislocations, horizontal height, parallaxes of motion, are important here in some detail. All these constitutive elements of spatial organization play their decisive role in the perceptive and cognitive comprehension of spatial stimuli which are referred to anticipating dispositions in a suitably contextual manner, relative to the observer based on aspects of main invariances such as size, form, coloring and localization of objects.

It is sufficiently straightforward to suppose that all these elements listed here provide an explicit format for the mentality of those who are socialized within hodological spaces. Hence, it has been tried to construct these spaces according to aesthetical criteria in order to stimulate desired actions by initiating catalyzing life styles. The idea is that life styles are always expressive in the sense that they are subject to enacting. In the terminology of Pierre Bourdieu this is what the concept of *habitus* implies: characterized by a special sort of "capital" and the field of interactions in which this capital unfolds its activities within a given social praxis (cf. also Funke, Wassmann, 1999/2000 and http://www.psychologie.uni-heidelberg.de/ae/allg/lehre/ethn/ws99_rz_plan.html, especially: 55sqq.). Visualized this way, the everyday world is a *structure of articulation* in the first place (Funke, Wassmann, 1999/2000: 61,77). In particular, the appropriation of space during the first socialization period of children functions very much as the reading of traces, of social traces which mediate the semiotic charge a space carries. In this sense, we deal with the reading of traces of the aforementioned articulation which is already intrinsic to experienced space (Funke, Wassmann, 1999/2000: 85sqq.).

The important point is that this physiologically founded disposition for the spatialization of cognitive object relations which in the end triggers a permanent constructive activity of human reflexion according to given spatial criteria, develops to such all-encompassing universality that after all, (almost) *all possible conceptualizations of human reflexion are being spatialized* in the end. Even the rhythmical tact sequence of taking the environment in sight repeatedly in order to scan it with respect to possible alterations (a procedure whose result we call *time*) will be represented as a spatialized dimension with its own space axis. And in fact, next to time as coordinate, all possible entities of life are represented in terms of abstract space axes. In Bourdieu, e.g., we have primarily the abstract dimensions *functional division of labour, distribution of power, institutional differentiation* (Bourdieu, 1982, 2nd edition 1983: 212, 277sqq—Les Editions de Minuit, Paris, 1979).

A more recent example for a possible construction of space is the aesthetical plan of the settlement *Mariposa* (on Teneriffa). This project can be visualized as an approximation of a modernized *polis* conception: "Mariposa is not Greek space. It is imaginary and catches a more wordly culture—but it is a world culture which is fitted to the *human measure* provided by the Greek. Nobody knows why the Greek started one day to diminish the much more spectacular dimensions of the Egypt and Minoic cultures, why their architects suddenly ignored cyclopic measures of columns and pathways and created new measures of build-ings that reintegrated again into daily life instead of being simply grand. And in this sense, in Mariposa, one remembers spontaneously the Greek space as assembly of locations." (Knodt, 2006; www.reinhardt-knodt. de/text_mariposa. html [our emphasis]—see also more recently Thorhauer, 2008) And Knodt con-tinues: "What does it mean that space is an assembly of locations? It means that it is not the Euclidean space that governs. Which is that space of which Descartes tells us that it is equally extended into all directions. In the topological space of Aristotle however not one location is like the other, and this is also true for the pathways... Mariposa appears to be a 'hodological' space, that is a space which consists of the most different pathways and path types such that the pathways are locations themselves ... In hodological spaces there are stairways and path-ways, marble streets and narrow steps, smooth and raw surfaces which offer the most manifold pavement to the foot" (Knodt, 2006; Thorhauer, 2008). (In the lan-guage of topoi one could say that the paths formerly visualized as morphisms become themselves objects of the category of locations.)

Now, leaving aside the mentioned competition between Euclid and Aristo-tle or Descartes and Aristotle as to that, we note here the importance of the already mentioned *space contrast*: The manifold within a given unity is in centre of cognitive interest. Knodt refers here even to an idea of Benjamin (without actually naming this author): "The pathways in Mariposa do not merely lead to some place, they actually mean something particular, they tempt, they seem to say—choose me!" (Knodt, 2006; Thorhauer, 2008). (This is indeed the equivalent of what Benjamin describes as the secret of space in his "Passages" when space whispers to the *flaneur*: "What may have happened within me?" (Benjamin, 1982: volume I: 527. The whole phrase: "The *'colportage* phenomenon of space' is the essential experience of the flaneur ... Space is blinking to the flaneur: Now, what may have happened within me?"). At the same time, Knodt relates his report to a general concept of garden which can be read within the context of the *polis metaphor*: "Of course, Mariposa is a garden which is experienced by walking. It is the space which unfolds while walking, through which one passes while experi-encing... It is a space which is gleaming by something mathematical rather than being burdened with stories. This something is what shines forth the precision of geometry on the one hand, but also sensuality on the other, that is, more than the reduced dimensionality of the geometrical. Hence, in so far this garden shall mean something, it is peculiarly open or undefined... And if one looks at the location in more detail, then within them again, a number of peculiar locations unfolds such that the underlying principle is being repeated... 'Pathways' one thinks at once, this is the space of pathways! But this is not true either, because we do not have a park nor a space of paths alone. We have the most abstract within the most concrete, a sort of happening which permanently reconciles spaces within each other, a kind of 'space within space within space...' which demands one thing in the first place—to live in it, to make it live" (Knodt, 2006).

It is quite obvious that we encounter here a new aspect: the *fractality* of this sort of space. Indeed, the hodological space is not simply a linear space, as we have seen earlier. Instead it is an *organized hierarchy of spaces*, and it depends decisively on the chosen perspective as to what this space actually means in detail. Hence, this kind of space is *self-similar*, and we may bear this in mind as a practical criterion for a space which can appear *livable*. (And again, we can think of what Mazzola calls the *Yoneda philosophy* which takes that into account when talking within the context of mathematical topoi.)

The first one to discuss the aspect of a fractal space contrast has been Benjamin who speaks in his terminology of the "labyrinthine effect" of urban space when referring to the streets of Paris: "The city is the realization of the ancient human dream of the labyrinth." (Benjamin, 1982, volume 1: 541). The labyrinth however evokes contradictory connotations: On the one hand Benjamin differs between the concept of the *route* and that of the *street*, especially in view of an underlying mythological difference, where the route relates to the aberration (the odyssey). (Note that Benjamin does not elaborate on the etymological difference of "labyrinth" and "maze".) In a sense, the labyrinth connotes the synthese of horror. (Benjamin, 1982, volume 1: 647 (par.)). The "street" however replaces this horror by the boring monotony of a line of asphalt. On the other hand, Benjamin notes the Paris custom of "living on the street": "The Parisians make their street to become an *interieur*" (Benjamin, 1982, volume 1: 531). This is actually the dialectic of the urban labyrinth: It is an aberration which is sublated however by means of its comfort which it evokes due to all these installations, the "street furniture", and the various stalls where people buy and sell. Indeed, this dialectic characterizes the basic structure of communication within urban space. The most important difference between communication on the countryside and communication in a city is that the transformation caused by the emergence of large metropolitan areas introduces the function of self-representation. As Poe would say: The human of the crowd offers him/herself primarily as function to the alterity of the others, as an explicit service function indeed. It is exactly this aspect which comes into play in the famous paper of Engels, where he describes that the tendency towards centralization is reflecting the centralization of the capital (Engels, 1845: 254). He mentions especially London, which would have neither beginning nor ending, if one wandered across (Engels, 1845: 256 (par.)). Contrary to the Paris of the time however, London cannot evoke the comfort and livability which is provided by the *interieur* of its streets: Instead Engels reports of the actual isolation of the individuals (Engels, 1845: 257), and he continues: "The dissolution of humankind into monads of which each one possesses a particular purpose and a particular principle of life, the world of atoms is carried to extremes." Benjamin introduces the expression "space of life" and also "bios" (a word Foucault utilized later on, although with a stronger biological connotation). He proposes to structure this individual space by means of a personal map which would be capable of mapping the *lived Berlin* (or the lived Paris as to that, the formulation "Paris vécu" has been introduced by Léon Daudet), at least in its essential shape (Benjamin, 1970: 12sq.). He more or less refers then to the tradition of the 19th century *flaneur* who can be visualized as a kind of surveyor (and reporter) of urban space.

****

In order to close the argumentation now with respect to the formal part of the present enterprise, we will try to re-connect the aforementioned details to the topological aspects of space. We will do so on a comparatively more fundamental level than usual, because this will help to illustrate clearly as to what is the formal foundation of the relationship between cognition and communication on the one hand and space and network on the other as we have discussed it earlier.

What we will do here therefore, is to choose the viewpoint of Bounias as a starting point for re-formulating aspects of complexity theory and systems theory, and thereby demonstrating the relevance of the systems theory in the sense of Edgar Morin. (We follow here partially a revised formulation taken from Zimmermann, 2007a.) We thus assume from the beginning on that cognition is the product of a generative loop among the physical processes which lie at the foundation of both biological and anthropo-social processes, the latter being founded on the former, lying in turn at the foundation of the physical processes. *Communicated* cognition outlines the semiotic framework for the modeling of the world being represented by means of spaces exhibiting a specific topology which is equivalent to the appropriate representation of dynamical systems as well as to the connectivity of looped network structures.

First of all, we summarize shortly the main results of Bounias and his coworkers (Bounias, 1990; also Bounias & Bonaly, 2000). Under this perspective, life, as well as any kind of matter, is being embedded in mathematical spaces which is a formal advantage entailing a wide variety of possible fields of application as we have already seen when discussing topoi. And we have thus to look for means to produce sustaining concepts of spaces by studying the structure of these spaces. As far back as in the well-known book of Jantsch (1982: 297), it is the complexity of systems dynamics visualized as a mediation of organizational microlevels and macrolevels that is at the origin of the bio-molecular communication. From the beginning on, we will have to read therefore the ideas of Bounias in terms of "two registers", because there is some sort of onto-epistemic deficiency in this approach: We should rather re-formulate that *if models deal with mathematical spaces, then representations of life/matter can be such that both of them appear to embedded into a formal framework of that kind.* This differentiation of formulating is necessary in order to visualize physical properties of systems (and hence also biological properties) as a result of human cognition which is initializing the modeling in the first place and defines some sort of specific disposition with respect to the world. This is what we have called the "onto-epistemic" aspect (utilizing the terminology of Sandkuehler) earlier (Zimmermann, 1989; also Zimmermann, 1991a, 1991b, 1998, http://www.zynet.co.uk/imprint/Tuc-son/1.htm. Also in Zimmermann, 1999, 2004c, 2004a). As it turns out, correcting the formulations of Bounias with a view to the onto-epistemic principle contributes to the clarification of his own concepts indeed. Hence, in order to sustain the spaces involved, what we need then is a condition of localized similarity which implies a criterion of formal stability of what is being perceived. Note that the structures involved are of essentially classical nature such that the activity of modeling shows up here as a direct consequence of (human) cognition which relies on essentially classical approaches in the first place. In this sense, Bounias can formulate accordingly:

> The global planetary ecosystem and its subsystems have properties of a topological space (X, τ) where X is the set of biotic and abiotic members and τ a rule of combination such that interactions among the components of X are being mapped.

What is essentially described here is the (mathematical) category of ecosystems ECO, where the objects are *agents* and the morphisms are *interactions* among agents. (Remember the aspects of game theory we have mentioned so far.) We utilize here the terminology of (mathematical) category theory (or *topos theory* rather), because, as we shall see, this will prove useful for a unified presentation of the problems involved here. For the time being we will just remember oncemore that a *topos* is a Lindenbaum algebra for a logical theory whose models are the points of a space. In other words, we can visualize a whole theory by means of a space such that topologically, the open sets of that space are the propositional formulae and the sheafs are the predicate formulae. A continuous map is then nothing but a transformation of models that is definable within the geometric logic. (Such topoi are commonly referred to as *locales*.) For a recent general introduction see Lawvere and Rosebrugh (2003).

The basic assumption of Bounias then is that optimum properties (as to the worldly spaces as introduced above) can be arrived at iff the *space of orbits* of members of X under τ has appropriate topological properties (namely is compact & complete).

In order to understand the precise meaning of this formulation, we collect here some elementary definitions which can be easily related to the sort of mathematics which is usually learnt at school when dealing with simplified cases:

> *Embedding* = injective immersion (A differentiable mapping f is an *immersion* iff the set of germs of functions on the domain coincides with the reciprocal images under f of the germs of functions on the codomain.)

Germ (of a function) = equivalence class of functions which coincide in the neighborhood of some point. (Germs form an algebra and a vector space. A tangent vector is a derivation of the algebra of germs of differentiable functions.)

Topological Space (Topspace): Set S and $\{O\}$ collection of subsets of S called open sets. The latter satisfy essentially three conditions:

1. The union of any number of open sets is an open set.
2. The intersection of any number of open sets is an open set.
3. In particular, S and $\emptyset$ are open sets.

Limit point p of a subset $X \subset S$: every open set containing p also contains a point of X distinct from p. (Relevant for Hausdorff spaces in order to actually define points reasonably.)

Subset $X \subset S$ is *closed*, if $C(X)$ in S is open. *Closure* of X: $\mathrm{clo}(X) :=$ Union of X with all its limit points. If $X \subset S$, then X is closed iff $X = \mathrm{clo}(X)$.

Compact: S topspace, and if a finite subcollection of $\{O\}$ covers S. (A collection is a covering of S, if the union of all its sets conatins S.)

Complete: A subset of a top (vector-) space, if each Cauchy net converges to some point in it. (Sequence which is a Cauchy net is a *Cauchy sequence*.)

Every compact metric space is complete. A space homeomorphic to it is called topologically complete. (Note that completeness is orginally not a topological invariant.)

Fixed point $x \in S$: f self-mapping, then $f(x) = x$.

Poincaré sections: (space-time-like) non-linear convolutions of morphisms ($\Rightarrow$ space-time related to ordered perceptions of existence, not to existence itself).

Topological filter: Family of nonempty subspaces (ecosystems) whose properties are being conserved $\Rightarrow$ defines an order relation by inclusion $\Rightarrow$ ecosystem hierarchies (This is relevant for the epistemic side of Morin's systems theory!)

We can also show that any metric space M can be isometrically embedded in a complete metric space N such that M is dense in N ($N = \mathrm{clo}(M)$).

Hence, for Bounias, the sustainable future of the world relies on two conditions:

1. The maximization of complementarity in habitat occupation and resource ultilization, and;
2. The reciprocal contribution of subsystems (mutualism).

(Actually, Bounias can show that these conditions are such that the actual identification of an X implies the concrete possibility that a proposition P—of some theory *about* this world—is true.) Then an object is *physical*: if the interaction with others can be observed (on the condition that the object be topologically closed)—which relates the concepts of systems and forms with each other. And an object is *biological*: if there is *a self* generated by some "perception function" caused by perceptive input mapped essentially to one and the same entity (which is called a *terminal set*). This condition is indeed fulfilled by the actual existence of fixed points or parts in the neuronal sequences mapping that input. Hence, the *topology of brain space* may be metric or not (if time is visualized as derived from ordered sequences of Poincaré sections in the embedding space). We have then with Bounias the following two results (which we re-formulate at once according to the aforementioned principle):

Result 1: An ecosystem has properties of a mathematical space. [!] ⟺ Ecosystems are modeled such that they have properties of a mathematical space.

Result 2: The set of ecosystems can constitute a topological space. [!] ⟺ Topological models are such that they can constitute representations of sets of ecosystems.

(The re-formulations secure that the respective model property corresponds to the modality of the world which signifies a material property of the world's reality. This is nothing but a re-phrasing of Spinoza's celebrated "identity theorem" of his *Ethics* 2p7. We can utilize this instance to show how classical philosophy actually *does* enter science, but only in a post-hoc re-construction of formulations.)

So we can finally say what an ecosystem actually is for Bounias:

Ecosystem: X, set of living species E together with a set of nonliving entities including habitat and resources H, τ being interactions of all sorts (transformations of states) = manifold of self-mapping of $E \cup H$. (Structures of this sort are called *magmas* when Bounias possibly refers here to Castoriadis.)

We recognize from the appearance of Boolean logic that we are invited to replace the underlying Boolean algebra by an appropriate Heyting algebra in order to arrive at the topos terminology. We give one example in more detail:

The example deals with the representation of the *DNA structure* in terms of self-interactions of containers and extainers. This approach goes back to Louis Kauffman who is one of the leading protagonists of mathematical knot theory. (Boi, 2005; see also Kauffman, 2001) We follow here the argument taken from Kauffman 2002 (Boi, 2005a; Kauffmann, 2001, 2002, 2005 and also www.arXiv. org /pdf/math.QA/0105255 and www.arXiv.org/pdf/quant-ph/0204007 v2):

Be DNA = < > = C(container); and > < = E(extainer), then:

EE = > < > < = > C < ; CC = < > < > = < E >. Then also: DNA ⇒ < E > = CC = DNA DNA (double strands). Call the strands "Watson" and "Crick", respectively, then:

$$DNA = < W \mid C >.$$

Replication is organized following strand separation initialized by a polymerase enzyme. The basic pairs are AT and GC, thus, if

$$< W \mid = < ... \ TTAGAA \ ... \mid, \text{ then } \mid C > = \mid ... \ AATCTT \ ...>. \text{ Hence:}$$

$$< W \mid + \ E \Rightarrow < W \mid C > = DNA, \text{ and,}$$

$$E + \mid C> \ \Rightarrow < W \mid C > = DNA,$$

$$\text{with} < W \mid C > \ \Rightarrow <W \mid + \ E + \mid C > = < W \mid C > < W \mid C >.$$

Therefore, $E \Rightarrow \mid C > < W \mid$ represents the process by which the environment supplies complementary base pairs. *So* E *is the identity element in this algebra of cellular interaction.* This algebra is in fact a precursor of the Temperley-Lieb algebra which relates the Artin braid group with the Jones polynomial invariants of knots and links. And they in turn can be visualized as quantum computers:

$$cup := \mid a > : C \to V \otimes V \text{ (creation operator)}$$

$$cap := < b \mid : V \otimes V \to C \text{ (annihilation operator)}.$$

This defines a computation of a link amplitude ("state sum"):

$$Z_K = < cup \mid M \mid cap >$$

(M: braiding / unitary). The Jones polynomial plays a central role in quantum computation of the kind described here:

$$< K > := \Sigma_\sigma < K \mid s > d^{\|\sigma\|}.$$

This is not only a playful mathematical formalism: Instead, the algebraic aspects of what is shown here tell us that there is a close relationship between the biological structure of the DNA molecule and the physical processes underlying the organization of the world. This is mainly so, because the Jones polynomial can be utilized in demonstrating that quantum gravity (which signifies the most fundamental level of physics) is essentially equivalent to quantum computation. Hence, the exchange of information according to the aforementioned definition of Jantsch shows up here in terms of a communication taking place among fundamental physical agents (which are the spin networks in fact). And the biological structure of the DNA can be derived directly from the physical structure of that communication *without crossing chemistry explicitly*. It is the computation of link amplitudes of spin networks which can be shown to *actually produce* the biological structure (among others). This confirms the unifying role of a theory which strives for the foundations of biosemiotics!

On the other hand, we learn something important about the human production of signs: The meaning derived from essentially meaningless symbols (of containers and extainers) can be readily fitted into a productive context (in fact, probably into *any* such context) which serves as the conceptual base for developing a theory (Zimmermann, 2004a). This is a very useful demonstration of what we have called *onto-epistemic* earlier: The mere manipulation of symbolic, i.e., abstract, form *produces* an associative meaning which serves a theory built on associative abduction rather than on concrete deduction. (In semiotics, this has been an important insight of Umberto Eco's.)

In fact, it is Boi who can show that the action of the *topoisomerase* which is responsible for the DNA replication can be visualized as the cutting of the molecule, letting a strand pass through it and recombine. The single-strand molecule (type I) and the double-strand molecule (type II) can also be described as looping and tangling in a writhing process, which is due to a site-specific recombination called *recombinase*. There are combinatorial invariants then which obey the rule:

$$Lk(C1, C2) = Tw(B) + Wr(B),$$

where the C are the backbone curves of the closed strands and twist and writhing numbers refer to the ribbon B along the axis C. Here, Lk is the linking number. In other words, knots, catenanes, and also supercoiling are relevant for the DNA, but absent from RNA, polysaccharides, and lipids. Hence, the evolution of such knotting properties has essentially opened the way for the DNA to enfold an increasing number of components, hence to produce a *complex topology* of the molecule. In fact, most properties of the DNA are affected by closed circularity and the deformations associated with supercoiling (Zimmermann, 2004a: 246sq., 250, 264). Earlier Thom has already stressed the significance of topology for the evolution of biological forms (Thom, 1975, 1983. See also Zimmermann, 1988, 2001a, 2001b).

****

There is a large number of relationships between what we have said so far and the systemic approach of Edgar Morin who aims at a universal theory of hierarchically organized systems covering all fields of the world, as is expressed by the following symbolic diagrams: First of all, Morin makes clear that it is time to actually reconcile what has been separated before, namely *nature* from *culture*. (This is the motivation we have called *Spinozist* in this very text.) In this sense, also the difference between *homo faber* and *homo sapiens* on the one hand, and *homo demens* on the other, has to be reconciled. The first of the following diagrams of Morin's shall represent this intention including the dialectic mediation of the individual within society:

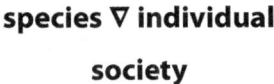

species ∇ individual

society

At the same time, this diagram symbolizes the (equally dialectically) interwoven network of micro- and microlevels. The second, methodological diagram is the following:

↺ Physics → Biology → Anthropo-Sociology ↻

This diagram symbolizes the looping mediation of the various fields of research. (We use here Morin's convention of depicting the loops such that those components which carry a loop at their side are being connected with each other within the diagram's completion.) However, this is not a static configuration, because all systems permanently re-generate and re-stabilize themselves by means of the organization of their (it-)self:

↺ Disorder → Interaction → Order → Organization ↻

This third diagram thus symbolizes the dynamical types of evolutionary processes involved. In principle, all three diagrams are also interwoven and steer thereby the processes of this world. (Morin, 1977: The German version of this book translated by ourselves is Morin, 2010). The underlying dynamical structure is of explicitly systemic kind. And *the system's structural skeleton* is the network of agent interactions. The important point is that also in the case of Morin's approach, the organizing centre of the processes is some self-activity, called the "Itself":

↺ Itself (se) ↻.

This dynamical nucleus is actually what organizes the generic aspects of the dynamical consequences of these processes. In this sense are they really *self-organizing* (to be more precise: they are actually *itself-organizing*). Indeed, this is the activity we may call *computation* in the strict sense: The brain computes, the mind cogitates, and the latter is emergent with respect to the former. The qualities related to this permanent procedure performed by brain and mind together are summarized in the following diagram:

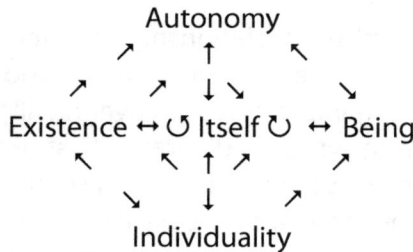

```
                     Autonomy
              ↗        ↑         ↖
        ↗        ↗  ↓ ↘              ↘
   Existence ↔ ↺ Itself ↻ ↔ Being
        ↖      ↖ ↑ ↗            ↗
              ↘      ↓      ↗
                  Individuality
```

On the other hand, this dynamical mediation is also coupled to the thermodynamic (thus classical) basis of processes given by the organizational hierarchy of the kind

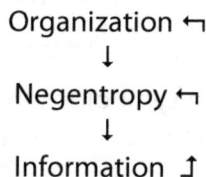

```
        Organization ↰
              ↓
        Negentropy ↰
              ↓
        Information ↱
```

which, by virtue of its productivity, initializes the generative loop, in which generativity itself is being inserted into the thermodynamical mediation:

$$\circlearrowleft \textbf{NEG} \rightarrow \textbf{GEN} \rightarrow \textbf{INF} \circlearrowright$$

In fact, what we really have here is a kind of commutative diagram in the sense that generativity is co-organizing with regeneration, because a self-loop is essentially recursive:

$$
\begin{array}{ccc}
\text{GEN} & \rightarrow & \text{INF} \\
\uparrow & & \downarrow \\
\text{NEG} & \leftarrow & \text{REG}
\end{array}
$$

We can give a number of conclusions now which follow from what we have said so far:

1. *Self-Reference of Systems*: There is an Itself as organizing centre of what becomes Self;

2. *Difference of System & Environment*: There is a hierarchical organizational structure of a system, and;

3. *Graphic Mediation of Modeling*: The cognitive aspect of process mediation secures the recognizability of graphical representations of systems.

In fact, magmas as abstract lattices in the sense of Bounias do actually guarantee the physical substratum (or *space*) ⇒ *cancelli sive spatium*. As we see this is very much on the line of what we mentioned with respect to Spinoza's approach! We can conclude that starting from perceptive aspects, experimental sciences give rise to theoretical descriptions of hidden features of the surrounding world. On the other hand, *mathematical proof theory* teaches us that any property of a given object must be consistent with the characteristics of the corresponding embedding space. As far as the looped representation of interactions is being concerned, we find a correspondence of the type:

Generative Loop (Morin) ⇔ Organizing Knots

(Louis Kauffman/Spencer-Brown)

This is indeed what *the abstract Kauffman scheme* does tell us: The boundary algebra of containers and extainers is to biologic what Boolean algebra is to classical logic. And more than that: Utilizing cellular automata for the simulation of lattice dynamics, we find that *shape* in general can be visualized as *memory space* according to Leyton (2001). This leads us back to what we have said in the beginning with respect to the role of biosemiotics according to Jantsch. We can indeed illustrate this aspect quite easily by utilizing Kauffman's knot theory in defining two ways of cutting knots (or unfolding them rather in the process of unknotting). Then we can re-construct the possible branches of the unknotting and define a *cognitive history of shape formation* by reversing the procedure

(Kauffman, 1993, 1995; as it turns out in the example chosen by Kauffman, we can recognize here a shape history for the simple case of the trefoil knot).

This has one more consequence to which Bounias has already alluded to when mentioning proof theory: As Carbone (2005) has shown, there is a structural analogy between the complementarity in formulae and logical connectives as used in proof theory and Watson-Crick complementarity of sequences (as we have discussed here in the first example). Proof theory proceeds with two principal rules (the contraction rule and the cut rule, respectively) such that a *formal proof* is a manipulation of sequences of formulae ending up with a sequence called theorem (Carbone, 2005: 387). In the process of elimination of cuts, the logical flow graph of a proof undergoes significant topological changes. And this points to the combinatorial idea underlying cut elimination: Given a logical graph of the proof, the procedure chooses a subgraph of it and resolves some of the focusing and defocusing points by duplicating it—which is obviously reminiscent of the enzyme recombinase in DNA as we have mentioned earlier (Carbone, 2005: 393). Note also that this is for the case of biology a similar argument after all than it is for the case of chemistry when applying the idea of Fontana's.

There is another interesting aspect to this: According to what we have said just now, logical flow graphs of formal proofs are equivalent to trees of derivation (Carbone, 2005: 390). And this relates the ideas displayed here to our earlier conception of a playable version of the *glass bead game* (Zimmermann, 2005a). The relevance is the following: because the essential problem of finding an adequate language for phrasing the foundational operations laying the grounds for biosemiotics is (as it is actually the case for all theories which are genuinely interdisciplinary) to find an "intermediate" set of lexicology, syntax, and semantics rather than utilizing nothing but specialized mathematical language. Hence, a playful language of simple rules for a logical game based primarily on the topology of two-dimensional graphs, for example, represents a comparatively promising approach. The idea of the glass bead game (visualized in terms of the conception discussed in the following section of this present text) is mainly to derive tree structures of the aforementioned kind and detect their bifurcation points, connectives to other planes of argument, count evolutionary steps, and so forth. Hence, the descriptive activity is essentially of combinatorial and topological kind. In particular, the consistency of propositions placed as tokens into the space of free play and their logical connectives shall be expressed in terms of the shape generated by this procedure, which is observable on the screen. Hence, this approach also provides a kind of formal correspondence between logical derivation and intuitive association of forms, thus of associative abduction, as we have mentioned it above.

CHAPTER 5

A Game-Theoretical Viewpoint (On Human Servitude, Or The Strength Of The Emotions)

In his novel *The Glass Bead Game*, Hermann Hesse introduces an essentially cosmic game within a symbolical universe which recently has been compared with a "neuronal network of the cosmic mind." (Cf. www.glassbeadgame. com—We follow here a revised version of our argument discussed in more detail in: Zimmermann, 2005a (prec. note)). In his game all those games which are known to us today appear to be summarized. On closer inspection, the glass bead game shows up as a *metagame*, a *proto-game* and a *playful paradigm of playing*. In its rules it encompasses the reflexive activity of humans within the worldly environment. It aims toward all those fields of the sciences and the arts which are available as the inventory of human orientation. "These rules" are, as Hesse explains, "the sign language and grammar of the game, representing a kind of highly developed secret language in which several sciences and arts, in particular mathematics and music (or the science of music) participate and are able to express the contents and results of practically all of the sciences and relate them to each other" (Hesse, 1943/1977, volume I: 12sq.; here and later always our own translation).

This systematic form of approach to a universal game, conceptualized in a global manner, implies an important methodological consequence. Hesse continues: "The glass bead game is thus a game with all the contents and the values of our culture. It plays with them, as in the heyday of the arts a painter may have played with the colors on his palette. What humankind has produced in its creative epochs in terms of knowledge, noble thoughts and works of art, what the successive epochs of learned reflection have conceptualized and claimed as intellectual property, all of this extraordinary material of intellectual values is being played by the glass bead player like an organ is played by the organist, and this organ is of a hardly graspable perfection. Its manuals and pedals are scanning the whole spiritual cosmos. Its registers are almost uncountable. Theoretically, the complete intellectual contents of the world could be reproduced by playing."

Today, the idea of such a playful simulation of the world has become more common than in the time of Hesse himself. Our modern attitude to visualize the world in strict analogy with a computer, to utilize the *concept of the computer* itself as a guiding paradigm of grasping the world, facilitates the understanding of processes which emerge within a playful construction. The world appears to us as the programmed result of some matrix which relates to what we call "world" as a master program relates to a sub-routine. And the aspect of simulation is not a conceptual problem for us anymore, since we have learned that *all of our perception* is nothing but an interpretive mapping, so that the perceptive as well as cognitive work is very similar to the process of simulation. There is no question of an eventually restricted authenticity anymore and no question of an ontological proof for the existence of human consciousness. Of course, the computer as a paradigm is not somehow equal to those computers we are actually able to construct and built. Instead, it is the *structural concept of a computer* which serves as an orientation. The same is true for the generalization of the concept of "program," because a program is less something which fixes what can be actualized during its processing and, more the *framework of what can possibly actualized* at all. It is a "field of possibilities" from which the process can actually choose.

With a view to the organ metaphor, Hesse continues. "These manuals, pedals, and registers [of the organ] have been fixed by now, and any changes or attempts to perfect their number or order are possible only in theory. The enrichment of the game language by means of introducing new contents is delegated to the strictest control by the superior game's steering committee. But within this fixed construction or within the complex mechanics of this giant organ, the single player is given a whole world of possibilities and combinations, and among a thousand games performed according to the rules, for only two of them to be more similar to each other than merely at their surface is practically outside the range of possibility. Even if it happened once by coincidence that two players chose the same selection of topics as contents of the game, these two games would look and run completely differently according to the style of thinking, the character, the mood and the virtuosity of the player" (Hesse, 1943/1977, volume I: 12).

As Hesse describes in his novel the glass bead game as the result of a long development, he sheds some light on the sciences and arts as they are available to us today exhibiting a permanent striving for epistemic unity. "Each attempt to approach the unity of the exact and of the more liberal sciences, each attempt to reconcile science and art or science and religion, is based on the same eternal idea which has gained its shape for us in the glass bead game" (Hesse, 1943/1977, volume 1: 13).

Hesse does not even flinch from introducing those fields of human thinking into the game which cannot be grasped and expressed in clear communicative terms of some linguistic discourse, as is otherwise the case for the sciences and most of the arts. He states, "As the glass bead game had been grown from its beginning in terms of technique and scope up to the infinite, and had become a high art and science in itself, as far as the intellectual claim of the player is concerned, there was nevertheless something missing. Up to then, in fact, each game had been a chaining, ordering, grouping and confronting of concentrated ideas from many fields of thinking and of beauty, a quick remembering of eternal values and forms, a short masterly flight through the empires of the mind. It was not until considerably later that, from the intellectual inventory of the educational system and from the habits and customs of the Riders of the East, the concept of contemplation came into play. This was the turn against the religious. It was not anymore the point to simply follow the series of ideas and the complete spiritual mosaic of a game with alert concentration and practiced memory in an intellectual manner. Now the demand emerged for a deeper and emotional devotion. After each sign was conjured up by the director of the game it was made the object of strict and silent consideration in terms of its contents, origin, and sense, which forced every player to make the sign's aspects intensively and organically present. The technique and practice of contemplation was exercised by all members of the order and the playing guilds from the élite schools where the art of contemplating and meditating was attended to with greatest care. This was the reason for saving the hieroglyphs of the game from degenerating into mere letters" (Hesse, 1943/1977, volume I: 37sq.).

The game shows up as a process which unfolds under two chief aspects, the one aiming at the universal which is part of the social collective, the other aiming at the singular which is represented by the individual. The first aspect refers to the constellations of thinking which are transported by cultural tradition. "In the designations, keys, signatures and abbreviations of the game language a formula of astronomical mathematics, the form principle of an ancient sonata, and aphorism of Kungfutse and so forth had been stored. A reader who is not acquainted with the glass bead game can visualize such a scheme as being similar a game of chess, only with the meanings of the figures (pieces) and the possibilities of their interactions with each other multiplied and each figure (piece), constellation and move symbolically designed by the chosen configuration" (Hesse, 1943/1977, volume I: 130). The second aspect aims at the practical introspection of the person playing. "The formal game aimed at a harmony and an unbroken, formally perfect unity, as dense as possible to be composed by the material contents of each game, the mathematical, linguistic, musical and so forth. The psychological game, on the other hand, looked for the unity and harmony not so much according to choice, ordering, linking, chaining and confrontation of the contents, but more according to the meditation following each stage of the game onto which it put all its emphasis" (Hesse, 1943/1977, volume I: 210).

Hesse's game can thus be visualized as a *game of interpretation*, as a game of interpreting the world within the questionable, observable worldly. Even if the world permanently lends itself to an interpretation which is questionable, it is the concentrated and complete taking in sight which guarantees that interpretation is not being lost in the undeterminedly arbitrary. "We shall direct the attention to everything, because everything can be interpreted" (Hesse, 1943/1977, volume I: 82). And this interpreting, as the main activity of the primarily hermeneutically constituted human, shows up as the translation of what has been perceived into a human universal language. The search for the latter is another ancient project of humankind. "[To study the whole game from the beginning to the end means that] I work through each of its propositions, translate it from the game language back into its original language, into mathematics, into ornamentics, into Chinese, into Greek and so forth. [W]e have invented and expanded the glass bead game in the run of the centuries as a universal language and method in order to express all intellectual and artistic values and concepts and to bring them to a common measure" (Hesse, 1943/1977, volume I: 125). By bringing them to a common measure, a universal human measure is actually being referenced. If it is anthropological qualities which are made the object of action in the glass bead game, then we deal with the humans altogether. And if humans are subject to what within the worldly are the actions they are able to perceive, then the problem is their own positioning with respect to that which is perceived. It is the uncovering of the relationship between person and world and between person and human collective. By means of inserting oneself into the world and by means of communicating this with the others, the sense of the game unfolds and offers itself to interpretation. The world communicates with itself and utilizes humans as an organ of communication (Schelling). But the constitution of these humans is important. The conception of the game reflects the picture of the humans involved. "The human we mean and we would like to have, who is to become our objective, would be able to exchange every day his science or art with any of the others. In the glass bead game he would bring the most crystalline logic to light and within grammar the most creative phantasy" (Hesse, 1943/1977, volume I: 83). The game approaches a concrete utopia. "[The ideal,] the thought of the interior unity of all intellectual efforts of humans, the thought of universality, has found its perfect expression in our noble game" (Hesse, 1943/1977, volume I: 249).

When we ask today what remains of this literary conception of Hesse and what we can still utilize, we discover in the anthropological center of his ideas aiming at universality something which is still of importance, especially as far as the recent developments in the sciences and the arts concerned. Of course, we have to think of alterations in detail, because some of the concepts depend on the socialization of those who utilize them, and a straightforward translation is sometimes difficult, if not completely impossible. A central concept is *meditation*. It should be difficult to find a satisfactory answer as to its universal meaning. We would prefer to actually replace this concept with that of *association*, which appears to be more universal in semantic terms. Association is obviously a permanently present constituens of our everyday life, particularly in the sciences and arts, where it is condensed to an epistemic means of knowledge and understanding. Also, association introduces the aspect of the coincidental which appears to be relevant for human thinking, by being able to spontaneously shed light on an otherwise hidden sense. If asking what an actually playable version of the glass bead game could be today,—presently a project in development indeed—then deterministic (logical, algorithmic, propositional) reflection and pre-reflexive (non-propositional) association will be fixed ingredients (In fact, in the internet one can find a large number of groups who apparently deal with the development of a playable version of the game. However, as far as we can recognize, all of these approaches are not quite satisfactory until now.). The route toward a concrete version (possibly arranged as a computer game) is long, however (Zimmermann & Wiedemann, 2010a, b).

The literary picture implies that the general intention of such a game is to approach the simulation, if not the emulation, of the all-encompassing process of producing knowledge in all possible fields. The *playing around* with concepts is in that case what is at the root of this process. (In principle, playing around with concepts is nothing but simulating possibilities.) And this procedure has to be completed in terms of Eco's *associative (creative) abduction*. In this sense, anthropologically founded *bricolage* (Lévi-Strauss) is the condition of effectively reducing complexity in order to find orientation within the world.

A concrete game procedure might be represented by an algorithm which is contaminated somehow by associative abduction. The idea to develop a proto-type game of this sort was to utilize a given inventory of propositions which covers a wide range of fields (This inventory is given in our (Zimmermann, 2004b) as an attached appendix which can be removed from the bulk of the book and read separately). Similar to a game of *Go*, the player has a lattice to his/her disposition in which pieces are laid out on intersection points of the lines (In the case of *Go* the lattice is quadratic. For the Glass Bead Game it is more practical to choose a hexagonal lattice, but this does not change anything in the game's principles). However, in the case of the Glass Bead Game the pieces are not neutrally black or white pieces. They are colored in various ways, and they do represent whole propositions (which can but might not come from the mentioned inventory). The colors mark the state of a proposition and its rank (as theorems, corollaries and so forth). Pieces (propositions) will be positioned at vertices of a network whose edges represent propositional connectives which follow the common logical syntax. Because characteristic connectives are implications, edges are directed and an appropriate arrow is attached to them. The whole conception is laid out in a timely manner in terms of a computer game such that the basic lattice is being generated on the screen and vertices as well as all their possible connections (edges to their neighbors) are activated by clicking on them. An active web of propositions is being produced which are logically connected and represent a part of a given theory. For different fields of knowledge the levels of the network which are hierarchically ordered can be changed. Between levels there are *bridge propositions* which signify the exact location of an interdisciplinary proposition leading from one level to the other (The original idea to play the game within a three-dimensional lattice (on the computer screen not even a technical problem) has been given up after a while because the orientation for the player is turns out to be very difficult due to the bias the lattice is subjected to because of the effects of perspective. The three-dimensional network has been replaced therefore by a number of two-dimensional networks which are related to each other in a hierarchical way such that transitions between the levels are possible. Hence, the original lattice can be approximated in a somewhat satisfactory manner).

If research processes are being visualized as games, then the objective is equally the permanence of the system involved (not so much of the individual agents constituting the system). Language games rely on the consensual structure of the system's underlying foundations of relevant references. *Defecting* in a game means actually dodging these foundations in one way or another. However, such a *research game* is primarily aiming at innovations. Defections can actually belong to the standard repertoire of such a game, though their performance is not really independent of any boundary conditions. But this does not change the optimal result as to appropriate strategies. As the "Axelrod tournaments" have clearly shown, optimality is secured if choosing the *tit-for-tat* strategy or its *generous* version (waiting for the second defection) (Szabó & Fáth, 2006).

As we see in the Appendix II in more detail, there are Nash equilibria for research games that define a unique payoff matrix such that the *production of ideas* can be visualized as a parallel to processes involving common replicator systems. Theorem 12 (App. II) is still valid and prepares the route toward a quantity we can legitimately call *average fitness* (of the idea). Of course, "idea" is shorthand for "conceptualization of a given research problem." The evolution of concepts satisfies an analogue to the selection equation. So for a system that propagates research in a language game, it is equally true that the relevant research strategy attempts to approximate a strategy that is evolutionarily stable under the given constraints. The constraints correspond to epistemological foundations. This is what signifies a true *innovation*, because it implies that a new idea (which is a sort of mutant) can only enter the body of already available ideas, if its existence adds to the evolutionary stability of the system. In the sciences, this is achieved by means of consistency requirements, one of which is that the new idea has to be capable of incorporating the system of old ideas as special cases. The innovative input is generally achieved by rational individual players *representing* the research community which unfolds its appropriate population dynamics. But the mediation of micro- as well as macrolevels (individuals vs. population) is being reproduced in this approach to games, as is the mediation of both triads, which have been shown earlier to be characteristic of the explicit interaction between cognitive and communicative modes of behavior. It is also true that if the population has reached the optimal strategy which is evolutionarily stable, then the "mutant" idea can enter the population, only if it does not alter the average strategy of the system. In that case, it is time for a *change of paradigm* in the Kuhnian sense.

CHAPTER 6
Artificial Life Revisited

E ven in such a specialized field as general game theory (with a view to its epistemic foundations), we are still in the middle of discussing physical concepts which originate mainly in the process of conceptualizing physics rather than epistemology proper. Philosophy itself is primarily based on physical concepts, so it is useful to include a little excursion into the problems modern physics deals with, because they in turn are related to the systemic structure of the world, dealing after all with the emergence and complexity of evolutionary systems. This is something which directly connects the modeling of the world (in physical terms) with the modeling of artificial worlds, as is done in what the Sante Fe people call *artificial life*. (We have already discussed one example of this kind of approach: Kauffman's model of DNA replication.) As to the concepts of *emergence* and *complexity* which have become prominent in the sciences lately, the common opinion is to ascribe them to the human mode of cognitively modeling the physical world rather than to this world itself. In classical presentations of thermodynamics this aspect is usually based on a similar viewpoint as put forward by Boltzmann, for whom quantities such as temperature and entropy are chiefly macroscopic quantities only and cannot be actually found on the microscopic level proper. The temperature of a solid or fluid body or a gas shows up as observable quantity on the macroscopic level and can thus be easily measured, but on the molecular level it turns out to be equated with the average kinetic energy of the molecules constituting the body or gas of which the temperature is actually being measured: $\frac{1}{2}mc^2 = 3/2(Rm/M)T = (3/2)kT$, where c is the average velocity of the molecules, R is the gas constant, and M is the molar mass (Bergmann *et al.*, 1970; cf. also Sommerfeld, 1977 and in particular Crutchfield, 1994; Edmonds, 1999—We follow here the argument of Zimmermann, 2008). It is this formal equality that usually veils the fact that the temperature on the right-hand side belongs to a level which is macroscopic with respect to the left-hand side. "Temperature" is simply a conventional *name* for the measuring of a phenomenon which can be observed only in terms of a mean value. Humans are "shortsighted" and utilize the name for practical reasons. The concept of temperature is *emergent* with respect to the particle statistics actually producing a phenomenon (heat) that can be observed and measured by a quantity of that name. In turn, masses and velocities on their own molecular level are emergent concepts with respect to the next lower level of fundamental particles, and so forth, all the way down to quarks and leptons. The same attitude should be valid in principle, if visualizing the other quantities of classical thermodynamics which appear in the free energy expression $F = U - TS$, or in the free enthalpy expression $G = H - TS$. Among them is entropy. Under this systematic perspective, the concept of emergence is deeply connected to the concept of information. The state space representation replacing the configurational representation of classical thermodynamics leads to conceptualizing entropy within statistical physics as a state property and a measure of deficient knowledge rather than as observable (in the sense of operators on Hilbert spaces). This is consistent within the Boltzmannian viewpoint but not within Prigogine's approach. Prigogine tries to resolve the common debate on the contrast of reversibility and indeterminism of microscopic laws (including quantum theory) and irreversibility and determinism of macroscopic laws by advocating (contrary to Boltzmann) that irreversibility and entropy are not limited to macroscopic physics. For him, processes like the decay of an excited state contribute to the entropy balance as well. Moreover, contrary to Pauli, Prigogine purports that the symmetry between incoming and outgoing waves as used in S-matrix theory is broken, because the incoming waves have lower entropy. Finally, he tries to unify (sublate) the duality between reversible and irreversible processes introduced originally by von Neumann. The consequence is that *probability* does not emerge from supplementary approximations made because of lack of knowledge, but instead as a dynamical consequence of resonance singularities in non-integrable systems. (This is somehow reminiscent of the way Penrose introduced his twistor concept.) For Prigogine, irreversibility is formulated within a theory of transformations that expresses in explicit terms what the classical formulation of the dynamics tends to hide (Karpov *et al.*, 2003). Prigogine locates the reasons for the classical approach in the limitation to integrable systems. For these systems, there is a unitary transformation U which is distributive.

$$U(ab) = U(a)U(b)$$

But for *non-integrable* systems (which form the majority in nature), the unitary operator has to be replaced by a more general operator Λ called *star unitary* which is not distributive:

$$\Lambda(ab) \neq \Lambda(a)\Lambda(b)$$

From time evolution as a unitary group, we pass to Markovian dynamics by means of utilizing a Lyapunov variable $H := \Lambda^*\Lambda$ (the star indicating hermitian conjugacy). The operator Λ is displayed as giving rise to a *non-local* transformation which means that in the new representation, points are being replaced by ensembles. Contrary to Planck (in the Hilbert space representation) there is a microscopic formulation of thermodynamics now which includes decay and excitation of quantum states. Entropy creation is here due to a resonance in the time evolution. The Heisenberg evolution is:

$$H(t) = e^{iht} H e^{-iht} = e^{-2\gamma t} H, \gamma > 2$$

where h is the usual Hamiltonian. The expectation value of H decreases, and entropy increases as the energy of the excited state is transferred to the field modes.

In the language of density matrices, Prigogine replaces the common entropy functional $-k \operatorname{Tr} \rho \ln \rho$ by introducing a modified $\rho' = \Lambda^{-1}(L)\rho$ which is a superoperator on Hilbert space of the system in question defined as a function of the Liouville operator such that the von Neumann equation for ρ, namely $d\rho/dt = -iL\rho$, induces another equation of motion for ρ':

$$d\rho'/dt = -i\Lambda^{-1}(L)L\Lambda(L)\rho'$$

which defines a new entropy functional of the form $-k \operatorname{Tr} \rho' \ln \rho'$ (and which increases with time) (Beretta, 2008).

The roots of this approach were laid down as early as 1979, (see Prigogine, 1979, 1993, 1997) and it is astonishing to note that by doing so, Prigogine replaced unitarity with non-unitarity and actually left the representations of Hilbert space. He is able to discuss mixed systems in the sense that reversible and irreversible components of a generalized evolution operator can be unified such that the symmetry properties reproduce those of Boltzmann's equation. Not only is the underlying entropy operator of *microscopic* kind, but it can also be explicitly written as a product of some operator T with its hermitian adjoint such that T turns out to be equal to Λ^{-1} and can be interpreted as *time operator*. It can also be shown that macroscopic time is nothing but the mean value of this new time operator.

This can be understood when thinking of Prigogine's version of the uncertainty relation which involves the Liouville operator.

$$[L,T] = il$$

Define then the mean values <T> and <T²> by $\operatorname{Tr}(\rho^* T \rho)$ and $\operatorname{Tr}(\rho^* T^2 \rho)$. (Note that again, exceptionally, we utilize the star here for hermitian conjugates.) We find by the above uncertainty relation that:

$$d\langle T\rangle/dt = \operatorname{Tr}(\rho^* \rho) = \text{const}$$

Normalization such that the constant is 1 gives:

$$dt = d\langle T\rangle$$

In approaches to quantum gravity, notably to *loop quantum gravity*, the role of spin networks becomes relevant (Asthekar *et al.*, 2000). It is the edges of spin networks that pierce the horizon of black holes and by doing so excite curvature degrees of freedom on the surface. These excitations are microscopic states that account for the black hole entropy. We can find arguments in favour of visualizing a black hole as a device which is encoding quantum information (cf. Zizzi, 2000, 2003, 2006).

When discussing black holes, it is important to determine the appropriate density matrix on the physical part of Hilbert space which corresponds to the maximal entropy mixture of surface states for which the horizon area lies in this range. The respective entropy is then,

$$S_{bh} = - Tr(\rho_{bh} \ln \rho_{bh})$$

and thus,

$$S_{bh} = \ln N_{bh}$$

with N being the dimension of the black hole's Hilbert space, which is the number of physical surface states. Those states have to be counted and form a basis of that Hilbert space. Then, according to the computation shown in the quoted work of Ashtekar and coworkers, we find,

$$S_{bh} = \ln 2 / 4\pi\sqrt{3} \, \gamma l_p^2 a_0 + o(a_0)$$

If γ is set to $\ln 2 / \pi\sqrt{3}$ to give the Barbero-Immirzi parameter, then the Hawking-Bekenstein result is being reproduced. For the black hole temperature and entropy, we find in the standard approach

$$T = \hbar / 2\pi\kappa, \quad S = 1/4 l_p^2 a$$

Here, κ refers to the surface gravity, i.e., to that acceleration which is necessary to keep objects at the horizon, and a is the surface area of the black hole's horizon, while l_p refers to the Planck length. (For a general Kerr-Newman black hole, e.g., we would have $\kappa = (r_+ - r_-)/2(r_+^2 + a^2)$, where the r mean the two horizons $r_\pm = m \pm \sqrt{(m^2 - q^2 - a^2)}$ with m as mass, q as electric charge, and a as angular momentum. The area is $A = 8\pi m[m + \sqrt{(m^2 - q^2 - a^2)}]$, and the entropy is $S = (2\pi k/h)[m + \sqrt{(m^2 - q^2 - a^2)}]$. Wheeler's "It-from-Bit" philosophy purports that the dominant contribution to entropy comes from states in which there is a very large number of punctures, each labelled by $j = \frac{1}{2}$ (half spin) and a $= \pm 1$. This has been generalized with respect to quantum computation by Paola Zizzi. Asthekar and others conclude from this that "[e]ntropy thus depends on the division of spacetime into exterior and interior regions, and is not an intrinsic attribute of spacetime. It is tied to the class of observers who live in the exterior region and for whom the isolated horizon is a physical boundary that separates the part they can access from that they cannot" (Asthekar *et al.*, 2000: 58).

If we follow (Stuart) Kauffman's viewpoint of visualizing processes in nature as *cooperative games of universal autonomous agents*, then the underlying entropy concept leads to a generalization of the thermodynamic laws. Following Kauffman's idea, we think of *agents* as systems which achieve a new kind of closure in a given space of catalytic and work tasks propagating work out of non-equilibrium states and playing natural games according to the constraints of their environment (Kauffman, S., 2000—The definition of agents is referring to an earlier manuscript version of the book which can be accessed under the address: www.santafe.edu/sfi/People/kauffman/Investigations.html. In the actual book version autonomous agents are defined as systems which can at least perform one thermodynamic work cycle). (Physical) space is visualized as being comprised of autocatalytic autonomous Planck scale agents coevolving with each other serving at the same time as some sort of crystallization of seeds of classicity. (Obviously, this view has not become explicit part of the book version, but without doubt this idea is still in the background of ongoing discussion.) This coevolution is taking place according to what Kauffman calls the *4th law of thermodynamics*: The maximum growth of the adjacent possible in the flow of a non-ergodic universe maximizes the rate of decoherence and the emergence of classicity. There is also a hierarchy of such agents depending on the explicit complexity of those in question ("higher-order agents") such that *human agents* in particular (as components of social systems) represent a stage of higher complexity as compared to physical, chemical or biological systems. But on the fundamental level of physics, Kauffman mentions the possibility to visualize *spin networks* as knots acting on knots to create knots in rich coupled cycles not unlike a metabolism. They (or their constituents) show up as "fundamental agents" of sorts.

If we take up this viewpoint, it appears to be straightforward to find the fundamental agents in the loops proper of *loop quantum gravity* (and the associated *quantum information theory*), which is consistent with Zizzi's approach. It is the loops which combine in order to form spin networks. By *loop* we mean a closed curve α such that $T[\alpha] = - \operatorname{Tr}[U_\alpha]$, where

$$U_\alpha(s_1, s_2) \sim P \exp\left\{ \int_{s_1}^{s_2} A_\alpha(\alpha(s)) ds \right\}$$

is the parallel propagator of A_a along α defined by (the s_i being points of α)

$$\frac{dU_\alpha(1,s)}{ds} = \frac{da_i(s)}{ds} A_i(i(s)) U_\alpha(1,s)$$

The SO(3)-field A is the difference of the SU(2)-spin connection and the extrinsic 3-curvature called *real Ashtekar connection*:

$$A_i^j(x) = \Gamma_i^j(x) - k_i^j(x)$$

The important result (cf. Rovelli) is that each spin network state can be decomposed into a finite linear combination of products of loop states.

Our conjecture is that *loops are universal agents*. Six of them, recombine to give one compartment of the hexagonal structure spanned by the spin networks. The conceptual reason for this is that the associated entropy satisfies the criterion for a thermodynamic cycle process such that,

$$1/4l_p^2 \int da \leq 0$$

where the integral is a closed path integral and a is the surface area generated with respect to one hexagonal fragment of the spin network. By the definition of loops above we clearly recognize that this procedure is not referring to some physically "vacuous" geometrical meaning, but that instead, this geometrical picture is physically loaded due to the parallel propagator with its gravitational or curvature connotation and the explicit group action involved.

This bears a strong resemblance to the Wilson loop representation (reminding us of the *loop transport* according to Stuart Kauffman's idea of agents), and is also a Feynman-type integral which gives the probability for a (physical) system to go from one state to another.

$$\langle x_2, t_2 \mid x_1, t_1 \rangle = \int_{x_1}^{x_n} D(x(t))e^{i/\hbar S}$$

where S is the action of the form,

$$S := \int_{t_1}^{t_2} dt L(x, x')$$

(The probability is the above expression squared. This is equivalent to the Schroedinger picture of quantum physics and a model for quantum computation.) As Freidel and Krasnov (1999) as well as Reisenberger and Rovelli (2000) have shown, spin networks and spin foams can be visualized as Feynman integrals such that the formal Feynman perturbation series of the partition function

$$Z = \int D\phi e^{-S[\phi]}$$

is given by,

$$Z = \sum_J N(J) \sum_e \prod_{f \in J} \dim a_f \prod_v A_v(e)$$

where J is a 2-complex, and the vertices, edges and faces are labelled accordingly. It is $N(J)$ the number of vertices of J divided by the number of symmetries of J.

There fare numerous important cross-relationships which connect the notion of loops with the notion of knots. Louis Kauffman's bracket algebra (the boundary algebra of containers and extainers) turns out to be the precursor of the Temperley-Lieb algebra important in order to construct representations of the Artin braid group related to the Jones polynomial in the theory of knot invariants. As the elementary bracket algebra is to *biologic* what Boolean logic is to classical logic, this has important epistemological consequences (on whose biosemiotic aspects I have reported in Salzburg last year. (Zimmermann, 2007a, in this section we repeat shortly the formal aspects of the quantum computer paradigm which have been presented earlier in this text.) The Jones polynomial can be visualized in terms of quantum computers because of a similar partition function of the form $Z_K = \langle \text{cup} \,|\, M \,|\, \text{cap} \rangle$ with creation and annihilation operations.

$$\text{cup} := |a\rangle : C \to V \otimes V,$$
$$\text{cap} := \langle b| : V \otimes V \to C,$$

M being the braiding, and $\langle K \rangle := \sum_\sigma \langle K \,|\, \sigma \rangle d^{\|\sigma\|}$ being related to the process of quantum computation (similar to spin network formalism). As spin networks are nothing but graphs, the *agency* in question is motion on graphs or percolation in networks such that phase transitions can be represented in terms of an appropriate cluster formation of connected components. This also points toward a close relationship to cellular automata utilized for the simulation of evolutionary processes (cf. Conway's game of life). Stuart Kauffman has associated this with the emergence of collectively autocatalytic sets of polymers and in fact with the onset of forming classicity with regards to physics. It is straightforward (in epistemic terms) to generalize this (with a view to higher-order agents) to chemical, biological and other systems. This is very much in line with Zizzi's arguments.

Utilizing the "skeleton-of-the-universe" view as described in our DPG spring conference talk (Berlin 2005) for the first time, (published in Zimmermann, 2007d) the idea would be to insert various steps of a hierarchy of complexity in the overall functor diagram from topological quantum field theory (cf. John Baez).

$$
\begin{array}{ccc}
n\text{Cob} & \to & \text{Hilb} \\[4pt]
\uparrow em & & \uparrow\downarrow id \\[4pt]
\text{SpinF} & \to & \text{Hilb.}
\end{array}
$$

This diagram is commutative, if an adequate emergence (em) mapping is being defined. SpinF is the category of spin foams, and nCob is the category of n-dimensional cobordisms. (For the time being, we can safely set $n = 4$.)

What is actually being confronted when comparing the above-mentioned approaches is the idea (as in classical thermodynamics as well as loop quantum gravity indicating the most fundamental level of physics) that the hierarchically ordered "averaging out" of indeterministic and reversible phenomena on the small scale is producing well-determined and irreversible phenomena on the large scale of the physical world and the different idea (as in Prigogine's approach) that, even on the lowest accessible level of the physical world, there is a concrete and active mixture of deterministic and indeterministic processes such that even intrinsically unstable fluctuations can actually create and determine large-scale phenomena. The first is a chiefly *epistemological* argument which ties the results obtained to the method applied. This can be visualized as an almost Spinozist viewpoint. The second is a more *ontological* argument detecting a creative potential of nature itself on its most fundamental level which ties the results obtained to some objective "form of being." This can be visualized as a Bergsonian viewpoint. The first entails the "metaphysical" idea that knowledge will be permanently increased and phenomena will become more and more observable. The second entails that on the microlevel, phenomena are non-observable in principle. The mentioned philosophers, and those who derived their approaches from one or the other influenced various scientists belonging to one of the groups. It is Prigogine who draws heavily on the ideas of Bergson, who in turn was known for his famous debate with Einstein on that point. In recent research we find various strings of argument which favor the first viewpoint or, equally, the second, according to the long-term perspective taken. Whether something can be observed or not *in principle* is decided according to whether one takes the strict opinion that true observation can only be based on sensory perception or the generalized opinion that observation encompasses all that instruments can actually measure, and if so, whether observation is objective or not. (Let us attribute the latter conviction to the classical viewpoint.)

The classical viewpoint makes clear that what can be observed (and known) depends on the evolutionary (and transitory) state of human knowledge, while Prigogine would argue instead that knowledge is limited *in principle* because some details of nature are not yet settled by nature itself. (This is an argument which places Prigogine in the vicinity of the philosopher Ernst Bloch.) The technical arguments involved are equally elegant, which is particularly obvious when discussing the most fundamental level of physics, that of quantum gravity. On that level, the introduction of an explicit reference to human knowledge gains a global kind of cosmological relevance.

There is, however, a major conceptual difficulty in the arguments of both viewpoints. In some way we would like to agree with both of them, contrary to their own arguments. Given the fact that human sensory perception is incomplete, we have no choice but to share the position taken by Prigogine. This is mainly because we do not want to agree to the assumption that instruments are merely means of "generalized sensory perception." Instead we would argue that they are constructed within the frame of reference given by existing theories. This also implies that observations are subjective in the anthropological sense. We share Kuhn's conception dealing with paradigms (Zimmermann, 2006; see also in some detail Zimmermann, 2005a, 2005b). This implies "architectural" consequences as to the relationship between the theories developed and the phenomena observed (Sambasivam & Bodas, 2006; Majima & Suzuki, 2005). On the other hand, taking this for granted, it does not entail anything which would speak against the viewpoint of "averages". We could also agree with the classical position with respect to averages.

	Epistemological view	Ontological view
	(Boltzmann, Ashtekar, etc.)	(Prigogine, etc.)
Macrophysics	Irreversible, deterministic average observable	Mixture observable
Microphysics	Reversible, indeterministic details partially observable	Mixture non-observable
Metaphysical frame of reference	Entails increasing observability	Entails non-observability in principle

Even if human beings might be able one day to possess complete knowledge with respect to their frame of reference which is determined by their biological capacity of sensory perceptions and including the development of instruments, their knowledge will only partly describe the world *as it really is*. We favor the viewpoint of Prigogine *while arguing ontologically*, but this does not necessarily imply Prigogine's conclusion on the relationship between what is observable and what is non-observable, because he refers to internal knowledge (within the interior of the world) rather than to external knowledge (of the world altogether). But we favor the classical viewpoint *while arguing epistemologically*. Our position is rather a compromise. We can call it *onto-epistemological* (Sandkuehler), and we refute the classical viewpoint of an objective knowledge which can be eventually completed.

A scientific compromise might offer Kauffman's approach. If we accept his viewpoint, then all he says is compatible with the idea of humans being complex agents organized in complex communities of agents playing natural games which in their case specialize to *social* games and are called meaningful. The cognitive activity of humans then, thinking and modelling the world, is a complex activity defined according to their complexity as agents. Humans show up as collectives of fundamental agents which coevolve in an organized community. A social system is a community of communities then. (This viewpoint is also compatible with the evolutionary theory of systems according to Edgar Morin.) We notice that this is *itself* the outcome of the modelling procedure. The systematic approach outlined above is nothing but another model among models, a mapping of the world, not the world itself. We utilize the concepts of *space*, *network*, and *system* according to our epistemological principles. Networks serve as a formal skeleton for a space and for a system while they are graphical representations of both of them. The concept of space serves also the graphical representation of what we call a system. The system is the concept we have of what we are able to observe in concrete terms. But what we observe is only part of the world. (Our ontological directive is: The world is not as we observe it.) *But we are products of that world ourselves*. There is the necessity of a *cognitive metatheory* for all of our other theories, which tells us something about the basic limitations of our possible knowledge and also about the necessity of a self-loop. Humans model the world by inventing theories according to the cognitive constraints this same world is imposing upon humans. Theories constitute categories of meaning. If humans show up as communities of communities of fundamental (natural) agents, they are *emergent structures* in nature, and so are all of their reflexive concepts. The concept of (human) meaning itself is emergent with respect to fundamental *proto-meaning* defined in terms of the directed behavior of fundamental agents in their (directed) fundamental networks of interaction. The consciousness necessary for reflection shows up as a human achievement, but on the fundamental level loops as agents may be interpreted as those who encounter the first (proto-) Big Wow—which in that case would be linked directly to the emergence of the Universe rather than to a later inflationary period, unless one reserves Zizzi's expression for the bit period proper.

CHAPTER 7

Ethics And Design (Concerning The Power Of The Intellect, Or, On Human Freedom)

Now, in reality, the most important (and most interesting) application of approaches of the kind we have discussed in detail here is one which centers around social systems. Is it possible to utilize topological and/or geometrical principles of harmony (as we have introduced them here in a more symbolical setting) in order to establish situations in a social system that guarantee sufficiently stable configurations of equilibrium? Visualized as a first conjecture, it appears to be straightforward to model such systems with a view to properties of categories (topoi especially) with the objects being concrete persons who constitute the social system (as individuals or as groups) and the morphisms being the interactions among them. This is the basic idea behind social network theory which emerged some time ago within the field of anthropological research. This is also what binds design science to Spinoza's idea of starting with physics and going up to politics after all.

The first attempt to formalize social group structures (possibly led by the straightforward analogy between social and mathematical concepts of *groups*) is probably André Weil's chapter XIV, written as an appendix to the first part of the famous work of Claude Lévi-Strauss: "The Elementary Structures of Kinship." (Lévi-Strauss, 1949. [Here referring to the English edition of 1969: app. p. 1, 221sqq.]). More recently, group theory has gained a prominent role in social network theory (cf. Boyd, 1979/80; Boyd & Everett, 1999; Freeman, 1996; White & Harary, 2000; White, Houseman, 2002). However, from the beginning there is a formal difficulty which clearly disturbs the formal consistency achieved. This is mainly due to the problem of compositions of mappings. Most papers related to this topic deal with descriptive or even trivial types of morphisms. John Boyd discusses social relations, in particular kinship relations, very much in the anthropological tradition. But in that case, although useful as an ordering conception, the results are describing and labelling rather than *interpreting* social interactions. If person A is the father of person B, then there is a relation $A \rightarrow B$ which is clearly defined and unique and cannot change over time. Without any doubt, if A and B live in the same family group (and in the same location), then there will be social interactions between A and B. But the fact that their relationship is well-defined will not tell anything about the *quality* of their interactions, even if some formal consequences are intrinsic. This difficulty is reflected in the notion of composition. Let us recall the definition of a mathematical category (refer to Appendix I).

A category C consists of:

1) A collection of objects Ob(C), and;

2) A set hom(x, y) of morphisms for each pair of objects x, y from x to y equipped with:

    a) an identity morphism of the form $1_x : x \to x$, and;

    b) a morphism $f \circ g: x \to z$ for each pair of morphisms $f: x \to y$, $g: y \to z$ called composition such that (i) for each morphism f the left and right laws of identity are valid: $1_x \circ f = f = f \circ 1_y$, and (ii) for each triple of morphisms the law of associativity is valid, that is: $(f \circ g) \circ h = f \circ (g \circ h)$.

The objects are the persons in a given social group and the morphisms are the social interactions among them. The identity morphisms can be consistently assumed because they are practically some sort of self-interactions. But note the composition: If (for reasons of simplicity) we reduce social interactions to pairwise verbal communication (linguistic discourse) between persons, then composition of morphisms according to the rules displayed above means that if f: $A \to B$ (A tells something to B on topic T) and g: $B \to C$ (B tells something to C on topic T), then this should be equal (in result) to $h = g \circ f: A \to C$. The identities are not problematic. But unfortunately, in general, the latter results will not be equal, because it depends on the individual person that is speaking *how the communicated proposition is interpreted according to the context of the receiver. A, B*, and *C* have different dispositions with respect to what is being said, and it is crucially important whether A tells something to C or B tells something to C, mediating what A said. In the case of formal descriptors this is not really a problem. If the mapping → is of the type "is father of" or "is boss of" or "is teacher of," composition is associative. Unfortunately, in these cases we do not learn very much about the concrete interactions. But if the mapping → is of the more specific type "is suppressing" or "is inflicting damage to" or "is supporting," then we have in general no associative compositions at all. This is true even if the people involved talk about the same topic and give away the same information in almost the same wording.

This difficulty has been discussed in the relevant papers from the beginning. Boyd remarks that the utilization of mathematical tricks in order to overcome this difficulty strongly reduces the information gained such that the results approach triviality (Boyd, 1979/80, 94sq.). This is the reason that he argues in favor of utilizing semigroups rather than categories. He would like to use the universal semigroup of relations which is essentially the quotient of the free semigroup generated by the relations R in question and the subgroup under given congruences (equivalence relations). In that case, two strings of relations are equivalent if the corresponding compositions are equal and nonempty (Boyd, 1979/80, 101sq.). We are not quite convinced, however, that this will solve the problem.

In order to clarify this somewhat, we take an example which will be discussed in more detail elsewhere (Zimmermann, 2008c). It is taken from a novel scenario provided by Elizabeth George (2006) which has the advantage of giving a plausible construction of a social group interaction within a geographically isolated area of the city of London. But at the same time, it has the disadvantage of necessarily simplifying real-life interactions in empirical terms. For our purposes, though, a small fragment of this example will suffice. The plot is essentially a narrative of the evolution of an intrigue staged and enacted by the leader of a local youth gang which ends with the charging of the main protagonist, Joel Campbell, with murder. The idea is to describe the interactions taking place in the protagonist's family and circle of friends and enemies, given the specific character of the local environment (consisting of the two London districts of Kensal Town and West Kilburn, which are parts of North Kensington). What we have here is the example of the social interactions within a number of groups which produce a concrete result. On the other hand, the environment itself (together with its inhabitants) can be visualized as a social space which is acting upon the participants in the social network forming its "skeleton" (or "circulation"). To be more precise, we take a fragment of this scenario.

An important protagonist in this story is Stanley Hynds (called *The Blade*), the gang leader. Another protagonist is Ivan Weatherall, a street worker who organizes cultural events and poetry meetings with a number of young people from the district. Call Joel "J," Hynds "H," and Weatherall "W." Interactions take place among them, namely pairwise, of the form $J \leftrightarrow H, J \leftrightarrow W, H \leftrightarrow W$. The arrow with double heads indicates that active communication is two-sided, and it makes a difference whether one or the other direction is taken into account. For simplicity, we can take the predominant direction of interacting according to the degree of initiative. Then, we have $f: H \to J$ (that is, Hynds is exploiting Joel), $g: W \to J$ (Weatherall is supporting Joel, giving him occasion to write and read his own poems), and $h: H \leftrightarrow W$ (Although Hynds could suppress Weatherall at any time, he does not do so, because the discourse between both of them is in a state of unstable equilibrium.). In the various situations in the district, these three persons entertain a joint discourse which can be visualized as unified with respect to boundary conditions (referring to the everyday policy in the quarter) as well as topical contents. However, a composition of (communication) morphisms is practically not possible, because, in general, $g \circ h \neq f$. This is not even taking associativity into account.

This is mainly so because all these persons live in their individual contexts which are not objectively defined but depend on their specific interpretations. The interpretations are themselves strategies altogether. So Joel is embedded in a context which is determined by at least ten more persons: his grandmother Glory and her friend (both of them absent by now), his (deceased) father, his mother Carole (who lives in a psychiatric clinic), his aunt Kendra (mother's sister), his younger brother Toby, his older sister Vanessa, a school friend Hibah, his open enemy Neal, boyfriend of Hibah's, and Dix D'Court, boyfriend of his aunt. With all of them he entertains a specific discourse. In most of these communicational structures he is the passive partner who is subjected to activities which are not those he would like to perform. He is strongly inclined to interpret his position in the family as a substitute for the deceased father trying to stabilize the life of his brother and sister while pursuing appeasement strategies with respect to his (absent-minded) mother and his aunt. At least Kendra, Toby and Vanessa move in similar sub-networks (contexts). We realize that asking for structural principles of harmony within a categorical framework as applied to social groups turns out after all to be extremely difficult—not because the formal apparatus would be too complex, but because of the hermeneutic space of free play which entails what we call *the freedom of interpretation* of some person (to be more precise, the freedom of assigning an explicit meaning to a given situation). This is what we learn from the existential philosophy of Sartre, and this is what *existence* is ultimately all about.

Looking at one of Boyd's examples demonstrates the informality and curtness of a relation-oriented approach. He introduces four sets of people such that three of them are members of rival factions with 'respected' leaders and one is a group of weak or evil characters (as he says) that are hated by all others (Boyd, 1979/80: 108). He works with relations called "hate" and "respect." In principle, this is a situation which can also be utilized in order to describe the gang relations in our prior example, but the results are sparse. We cannot even define a unique type of hierarchy for our example because the hermeneutic context is missing, which demands a detailed discussion of the quality of the interactions involved. As far as category theory is concerned, this demands a complex labelling of morphisms.

One way out could be the introduction of *fuzzy* categories, in analogy to fuzzy set theory. It can be shown that if *Fuz* is the category with objects (A, α) such that A is a set and α is the index function for fuzzy sets in the interval $[0, 1]$, and with morphisms $f: (A, \alpha) \rightarrow (B, \beta)$ between sets A and B such that $\alpha(a) \leq \beta(f(a))$ for all $a \in A$, then there are equalizers, finite products and exponentials in *Fuz* as well as a terminal object. However, there is no (precise) subobject classifier. Hence, *Fuz* cannot be made a topos, but it can be called *weak topos*, provided two generalized conditions are being fulfilled (Xue-hai Yuan *et al.*, 2002: 292sq.) Categories have been utilized recently within a similar conception by providing a network analysis for organizational systems (Dekker, 2001, 2007). However, as they are mainly applied to hierarchical structures within a military ranking and classification procedure (which can alternatively be applied to industrial and other commercial institutions), the hermeneutic component is practically neglected. This might have to do with the objective defined in these works. The first goal is seen in the visualizing of communication and other relationships between people and/or groups by means of diagrams. The second goal is being described as to study the factors which influence relationships and correlations among them. The third goal is said to be the drawing out of implications of the relational data. The fourth goal is to make recommendations to improve communication and workflow within the organization (Dekker, 2001: 1). All four goals can only be achieved if the interactions are formalizable in the sense discussed earlier. The attributes applied are chiefly of the type "is supervisor to" or "has (command) distance x from Y." In that case it is possible in categorical terms to associate with each person some predicate p such that the person *believes* (estimates) himself to be in a specific state of the network N onto which p acts as a functor, which can be visualized then as an *accessibility* relation among possible worlds (Dekker, 2001: 11). The problem is to optimize this estimation. This situation is not too different from the case described in our example, because the selection of an adequate strategy given the escalating conflict in the quarter is indeed the main objective to be achieved. However, the assumptions are far more complex, because in the district's gang hierarchy multifarious contexts of persons overlap, producing a variety of rational and non-rational decisions, while in the military case discussed in the paper this complexity is strongly reduced due to the fact that it is always the highest-ranking superior who "interprets" explicit commands.

At most we could say that there is some sort of overlapping in lifestyles which eventually might make it possible to achieve a consistent composition of interaction morphisms *from time to time under favorable conditions*. This idea is quite prominent in recent approaches to intercultural communication. In that case we would talk of *overlapping* contexts, and communication could be successful at least within that zone of overlapping (cf. Loh *et al.* 2008). (The idea of overlapping would be that if we have morphisms of the type f, g, h as above, then the mapping is not from points to points between spaces of interpretation that reflect what is going on when persons A, B, and C talk to one another but rather from neighborhoods of these points to other neighborhoods. Hence, f: $A \rightarrow B$ would correspond to a mapping ϕ: $C(A) \rightarrow C(B)$ such that some U(p $\in$ C(A)) is mapped onto some $f(U(p \in C(A))) = V(q \in C(B))$, where C are the respective contexts of the persons A, B that serve as the framework for interpreting what is being said and U and V are neighborhoods of points within the respective contexts. Overlapping, then, if it exists, is defined in terms of some suitable U $\cap$ V. (In fact, contrary to both Loh and Mall, we would claim that for any two persons, there is always at least one such intersection.).

Nevertheless, despite these technical difficulties, we would strive for a result which could be visualized as an alternative (generalized) formulation of Vicker's result mentioned earlier. We would like to assume that *a (weak or fuzzy) topos is the Lindenbaum-Tarski (fuzzy) algebra of a (pre-scientific, i.e. fuzzy) logical theory whose models are the points of social space.* That is nothing but a conjecture and a research program, but it is at least a promising way out when dealing with complex social systems. Another possibility is Mazzola's *Yoneda philosophy*. Recall that the formal idea of this is to visualize a functor between categories as a system which expresses all the views among objects onto their own (source) category (Mazzola, 1995). A more recent example for this deals with collaborative improvisation in jazz music (Mazzola, 2008. In fact, this is a phenomenon which can also be found at scientific conferences with similar results: In that case, it is called *hand-waving technique*).

CHAPTER 8
Conclusions

What we have essentially tried here follows in fact an earlier motivation given by Mazzola. Some time ago he collected the characteristics of *Big Science* and claimed the necessity to carry these characteristics over to a theory of music, referring to an earlier quotation of Pierre Boulez (1995).

Starting from the totalizing conception of Spinoza, we are ready to develop a similar attitude for the rest of philosophy and the humanities in order to actually include all relevant fields of human creativity. This is what *ethics* in Spinoza's sense is all about in the end: to ask for *adequate behavior according to present knowledge*. As the variety of concrete situations in everyday life is multifarious, so must be the respective knowledge. Knowledge has to become *totalizing* in the sense that it covers all relevant fields of human (creative) activity equally well, because it is these fields which are at the roots of explicit principles and criteria serving as guidelines for adequate ethics.

Of course, the route towards a closed theory in the sense of Mazzola's definition of Big Science cannot be traveled by individuals whose capacity is clearly deficient with a view to the complexity of the problems involved. No single protagonist of the past or present can actually claim the all-encompassing validity of his approach. This is particularly obvious in the celebrated works of Bertalanffy. (For critical reviews and systematic modifications of the theory of Bertalanffy's see, e.g., Boje, 2004 (peace@peaceaware.com: See http://cbae.nmsu.edu/~ dboje/; also, Martin, 2003 and web-site: http://systems.open.ac.uk/ page.cfm? pageid=resourceBert). This is also true for similarly well-known actors on the scene of holistic approaches. However, what is important for us here is the *general attitude* taken by all of these protagonists toward the objective of eventually finding a unified way of describing a concrete mediation of sceptic and speculative philosophy so as to include an onto-epistemic panorama of the sciences and arts that is moreover able to provide some heuristic insight into formal procedures for an ethical praxis that appears to us as being optimally adequate, at least for the time being.

APPENDIX I

A Very Short Introduction to Categories

We summarize now some elementary definitions and properties concerning mathematical categories. (We follow here the terminology and convention of John Baez, put forward on his website when discussing categories [utilize the search function on this site] http://math.ucr.edu/home/baez/): A *category* C consists of:

1. A collection of objects $\text{Ob}(C)$, and;

2. A set $\hom(x, y)$ of *morphisms* for each pair of objects x, y from x to y equipped with:

    a. An identity morphism of the form $1_x : x \to x$, and;

    b. A morphism $f \circ g: x \to z$ for each pair of morphisms $f: x \to y$, $g: y \to z$ called *composition* such that:

        i. For each morphism f the left and right laws of identity are valid: $1_x \circ f = f = f \circ 1_y$, and;

        ii. For each triple of morphisms the law of associativity is valid: $(f \circ g) \circ h = f \circ (g \circ h)$.

In particular, an *isomorphism* is a morphism which has an inverse. Given categories C and D, a *functor* $F: C \to D$ consists then of:

1. A function $F: \text{Ob}(C) \to \text{Ob}(D)$, and;

2. A function $F: \hom(x, y) \to \hom(F(x), F(y))$ for each pair $(x, y) \in \text{Ob}(C)$ such that:

    a. F preserves identities: that is, for each object $x \in \text{Ob}(C)$, $F(1_x) = 1_{F(x)}$, and;

    b. F preserves compositions: that is, for each pair of morphisms f, g in C we have: $F(f \circ g) = F(f) \circ F(g)$.

Given two functors $F, G: C \to D$, then a *natural transformation* $\alpha: F \Rightarrow G$ consists of a function α which maps each object $x \in C$ to a morphism $\alpha_x: F(x) \to G(x)$ such that for each morphism $f: x \to y$ in C the following diagram commutes:

$$F(x) \xrightarrow{F(f)} F(y)$$

$$\downarrow \alpha_x \qquad \downarrow \alpha_y$$

$$G(x) \xrightarrow{G(f)} G(y).$$

It can be shown straightforwardly that identities, compositions and the law of associativity are being preserved for natural transformations. Given two functors, a *natural isomorphism* is a natural transformation which has an inverse. Insofar as a natural transformation is a natural isomorphism iff (if and only if) for each object $x \in C$ the morphism α_x is invertible. A functor $F: C \to D$ is an *equivalence*, if it has a weak inverse, i.e., a functor $G: D \to C$ such that there are natural isomorphisms $\alpha: FG \Rightarrow 1_C$ and $\beta: GF \Rightarrow 1_D$.

A *monoidal category* (or monoid) consists of:

1. A category M;
2. A functor called *tensor product*, of the form $\otimes: M \times M \to M$ with $\otimes(x, y) = x \otimes y$ and $\otimes(f, g) = f \otimes g$ for objects $x, y \in M$ and morphisms f, g in M;
3. An identity object $1 \in M$, and;
4. Natural isomorphisms called *associators*: $a_{x,y,z}: (x \otimes y) \otimes z \to x \otimes (y \otimes z)$ satisfying the left and right laws of identity: $1_x: 1 \otimes x \to x$, $r_x: x \otimes 1 \to x$, such that:

    a. The following diagram commutes for all objects $w, x, y, z \in M$ (Pentagon equation):

$$(w \otimes x) \otimes (y \otimes z)$$

$$\nearrow \qquad\qquad \searrow$$

$$((w \otimes x) \otimes y) \otimes z \qquad\qquad w \otimes (x \otimes (y \otimes z))$$

$$\searrow \qquad\qquad \nearrow$$

$$(w \otimes (x \otimes y)) \otimes z \quad \to \quad w \otimes ((x \otimes y) \otimes z)$$

   and;

    b. The triangle equations are valid, i.e., the following diagram commutes:

$$(x \otimes 1) \otimes y \to x \otimes (1 \otimes y)$$

$$\searrow \qquad \swarrow$$

$$x \otimes y.$$

(We skipped here the signifying of the respective associators on their arrows.)

Important is the *principle of duality*. This means the inversion of the directions of all arrows. For propositions of the type $f: a \to b$, $a = \operatorname{dom} f$, $h = g \circ f$ the duals are the propositions $f: b \to a$, $a = \operatorname{cod} f$, $h = f \circ g$. The principle states that if the proposition Σ is a consequence of given axioms, then so is the dual proposition Σ^*. Dual categories will be signified by an upper index "opp" (opposite).

If for two categories C, D the respective $\hom(x, y)$ are sets, then we say that if there are also two functors $F: C \rightarrow D$ and $G: D \rightarrow C$, category C is *left-adjoint* to D (or equivalently: G is *right-adjoint* to F ($F \dashv G$), if the functors $\mathrm{Hom}_D(F): C^{\mathrm{opp}} \times D \rightarrow$ Sets and $\mathrm{Hom}_C(G): C^{\mathrm{opp}} \times D \rightarrow$ Sets are mutually isomorphic. A *terminal object* 1 in a category C is an object which admits exactly one morphism from each object x of the form $!: x \rightarrow 1$. An *initial object* 0 is a terminal object in the category C^{opp}. A *quiver* is a pair $G = (A, V)$, where the elements of V are called *vertices* and the elements of A *arrows*. If each pair of vertices is at most top and bottom of one arrow, then the quiver is called *directed graph*. Obviously, the category of paths $P(G)$ has the paths themselves as its morphisms.

Given a quiver and a category C, and also a diagram D from $P(C)$, and given an object c in C, there is the constant diagram $[c]$, which associates with each vertex in C this very c and with each arrow the identity id_c. A natural transformation $[c] \rightarrow \Delta$ is called *cone on* Δ, written as $K(\Delta)$, while a natural transformation $\Delta \rightarrow [c]$ is called *co-cone on* D, written as $KK(\Delta)$. (In a cone all arrows which start from c have to commute with the arrows of the diagram. In a co-cone all arrows which end in c have to commute with the arrows of the diagram.) Then a *limit* of Δ is a terminal object in $K(\Delta)$. While a *co-limit* of Δ is an initial object in $KK(\Delta)$. If the diagram is a pair of the form $f: a \rightarrow c$, $g: b \rightarrow c$, then the limit is called *fibre product* or *pullback* of f, g. If the diagram is a pair of the form $f: c \rightarrow a$, $g: c \rightarrow b$, then the co-limit is called *fibre sum* or *pushout* of f, g. In particular, a category is called *finitely (co-) complete* iff it has (co-) limits for all finite diagrams.

For any category C the following propositions are equivalent:

1. C is finitely complete;
2. C has finite products and equalizers. (These are limits of pairs of arrows.), and;
3. C has a terminal object and pullbacks.

Hence, the dual is also valid:

1. C is finitely co-complete;
2. C has finite sums and co-equalizers, and;
3. C has an initial object and pushouts.

It is here where the subobject classifyer comes into play which serves as a categorial analogue for the characteristic functions of set theory. The direct way of defining this leads via sheaf theory:

Be M a partially ordered set: A function which associates with each $p \in M$ a set X_p and with each pair $p \leq q$ a mapping $X_{qp}: X_q \rightarrow X_p$ such that $X_{pp} = \mathrm{id}(X_p)$, and, whenever $p \leq q \leq r$, $X_{rp} = X_{qp} \circ X_{rq}$, is called *pre-sheaf X on M*. A *subobject K* then of the pre-sheaf X is essentially another pre-sheaf with a similar mapping, K_{qp} say, which is a restriction of X_{qp}. The collection of all pre-sheaves on a partially ordered set M is itself a category called Set^M. (This can be shown to be a topos, because pre-sheaves can be alternatively defined in terms of *sieves* which are nothing but collections of morphisms acting on objects of M such that compositions are being preserved. The important property of sieves is that they imply the existence of subobject classifyers which have the structure of Heyting algebras.) We can also formulate that the category of functors $C^{opp} \to$ Sets of a given category C is the category of pre-sheaves of C. Given then for some category C a morphism $f: H \to G$ in the category of pre-sheaves of C. Then we have:

1. It is f a monomorphism iff $Af: AH \to AG$ is injective for all objects A of C (the products meaning here "evaluation at A");

2. It is f an epimorphism, if Af is surjective, and;

3. It is f an isomorphism, if Af is bijective, respectively. Then we have the following important definition:

Given a complete category C which has a terminal object 1, then a monomorphism *true*: $1 \to W$ in C is called *subobject classifyer* iff, given some monomorphism $s: S \to X$ in C, there is a unique morphism $t: X \to W$ such that the diagram

$$S \xrightarrow{\sigma} X$$

$$\downarrow! \quad \downarrow\tau$$

$$1 \xrightarrow{\text{true}} \Omega$$

is a pullback. (Subobject classifyers are unique up to isomorphisms.) In this sense a subobject of X is an equivalence class of monomorphisms of type σ. If all subobjects of X represent a set for each object X in C, then this set is a pre-sheaf of C. A category is called *Cartesian closed* iff it has finite products and each of its elements is exponentiable, i.e., if the functor AX: Sets $\to$ Sets: $X \to A \times X$ has a right-adjoint. (This is particularly true for the category of sets called *Sets*. Then the respective functor is X^A: Sets $\to$ Sets: $X \to X^A$. And the "power set" represents the functor $X \to \hom(A \times X, X)$.)

For a category C the following groups of properties are equivalent:

1. C is Cartesian closed and has a subobject classifyer;

2. C is Cartesian closed, finitely co-complete, and has a subobject classifyer;

3. C has a terminal object and pullbacks, exponentials, and a subobject classifyer;

4. C has a terminal object and pullbacks, an initial object and pushouts, exponentials, and a subobject classifyer, and;

5. C is finitely complete and has power objects.

A category which has these equivalent groups of properties is called (elementary) topos. (In particular it can be shown that the category of pre-sheaves for some category C is a topos.) Functors between topoi that preserve limits, exponentials, and subobject classifyers are called *logical morphisms*.

Take a *site* which a pair (C, J) with J a Grothendieck topology on C (in which sheaves take the role of open sets in terms of classical topology), then a presheaf P in C is a *sheaf* iff for each sieve of J the canonical diagram is an equalizer. The category which is equivalent to the category of sheaves $\text{Sh}(C, J)$ is called *Grothendieck topos*. A Grothendieck topos is an elementary topos.

This is where logic enters again. We go back to the case of orderings. A *preorder* is a binary equivalence relation which is reflexive as well as transitive. It is called *partial order*, if it is also anti-symmetric (pRq, $qRp \Rightarrow p = q$). Instead of pRq we can alternatively write $p \subseteq q$ such that a power set can be expressed by $P = (P, \subseteq)$. We call a power set which can be defined in terms of partial order a *lattice*. For any $x, y \in P$ the products $x \cap y$ and $x \cup y$ are called *meet* and *join*, respectively. The first case is meant to be the greatest lower bound, the second the least upper bound of x and y in the sense of a subset filtering. A lattice is called *bounded*, if there is some y complementary to x such that $x \cup y = 1 \wedge x \cup y = 0$. A bounded lattice is called *complemented*, if for each of its elements there is a complementary one within the lattice. A lattice is called *distributive*, if for each element there is at most one complementary element. In fact, the operations $\cap$ (meet), $\cup$ (join) and "complementarization" represent in the case of the set of truth values 2 the operations conjunction, disjunction, and negation (including implication). Hence, we can rewrite algebraic expressions as logic expressions such that diagrams commute; e.g. for the case of negation we have:

$$1^{\text{false}} \to 2$$

$$\downarrow \qquad \downarrow \neg$$

$$1^{\text{true}} \to 2$$

When passing over from Boolean to intuitionistic logic, then we have to take into account that the former is governed by Boolean algebras and the latter by Heyting algebras. The important difference between these two is in the negation operation. In the Boolean case negation shows up as "complementarization," similar to the case of duality: $\neg(\neg x) = x$. The negation of the negation reproduces the proposition again. In the case of a Heyting algebra, however, this is not true anymore. Instead, we have now: $\neg(\neg x) \neq x$. This means that recursive operations make the emergence of innovative structures possible. Categories become time-dependent, contrary to sets, because objects can be created as well as annihilated. (Already in the calculus of propositions can we find the consequences of this formal difference between the types of algebra (We have discussed the more elementary aspects of logic, especially with a view to the classical form of propositional calculus, e.g., with respect to the *modus ponens* elsewhere. See, e.g., Loh *et al.*, 2008: part 3.). The calculus of propositions deals with the evaluation ε of propositions of a given set (as mapping from this set onto a lattice A) in terms of their validity. A proposition a in this sense is *A-valid* iff $\varepsilon(\alpha) = 1$ ("true") under given rules. In the case of predicate logic the results of propositional calculus are being preserved (under appropriate generalizations and by introducing quantizing operators). We find that if $f\colon A \to B$ is a morphism in the topos C, then the functor $\mathrm{Sub}(B) \to \mathrm{Sub}(A)$ of Heyting algebras has a right-adjoint $\forall$ as well as a left-adjoint $\exists$. (Heyting algebras and thus intuitionistic logic is more generic for topos theory than Boolean classical logic.)

APPENDIX II
A Not So Very Short Introduction To Evolutionary Game Theory

In a modern interpretation of game theory which clearly transgresses the classic results of economic applications, the following aspects are relevant:

1. *The Dynamics of Populations*: In biology, species in view of populations of their individuals (phenotypes) are being treated as agents in competition with one another. On the simplest level of formalization, this competition can be described in terms of continuous mathematical models which are expressed by means of differential equations.

2. *Evolution*: This is visualized as an agent-based dynamic in a generalized sense as a dynamic of dynamics with respect to the species considered, where social groups of human beings are understood as special case.

3. *Competition and Game*: Each competition can be visualized as a game with definite results (winning, loosing, drawing).

4. *Natural and social games*: They do not differ by the structure of their respective organizations, but instead by the given constraints: the arena (space of free play), the rules, and the partners.

5. *Algorithms, Programs, Games*: The performance of a game can be compared with algorithms, i.e., with procedures which run from a starting point to a target whose strategies are defined by the rules. Algorithms can be represented by programs. All three of them show up as equivalents provided the assumptions are sufficiently simple.

6. *Algebraic Graphism of the Categories of Games*: An important recent insight is that games can be mapped onto mathematical categories which can be algebraically represented in terms of graphs. It is in this way that the dynamics of games are being reconciled with logic.

7. *Cooperative Games of Universal Autonomous Agents*: On the fundamental level of reflection it is the games of fundamental agents to be defined that constitute the processes of dynamic nature.

For simplicity, we restrict the sorts of games discussed here and refer to more recent results given by Robin Houston (2003). We assume that games are determined and their results are solely explained in terms of the strategies of the players. We also assume that there are exactly two players in a game who move one after the other in an alternating fashion. The state of the game is completely known to the players. The arena is the available space of free play which is independent of any other spatial location of the players (their position in physical space). The alternating moves imply that the time coordinate of the game is nothing but the succession of updates of the states of the game. (It is not necessarily identical to physical clock time.)

If strategies depend on the complete history of the game, we speak of *tree games*. Such games are similar to research strategies in the sciences. A *strategy* is simply a rule which prescribes the next move. Defining the *winning* of a game shows clearly the relationship between games and proof theoretic models of non-trivial logics. A strategy γ in game G (or in its associated arena) is said to win if each game which follows it ends in a p-position. The dual strategy is called *counter* strategy and ends in an o-position (p = player, o = opponent). We realize that all games of the type defined above are of a "planning" (or projective) type. (Well-known social games of this type are "chess" and "go." Their gain is usually either 1, 0 or ½ according to whether the game is won, lost or a draw.)

The strategy which leads from a starting point to a target can be understood as a route taken in abstract space. Winning strategies are optimal routes in that they minimize the distance between starting point and target. They can be represented by means of suitable graphs.

A *graph* in mathematics is a set (v, e) of vertices v and edges e. The latter connect the former with each other. Edges can be weighted by numbers in order to express their qualities. (If the vertices are persons/agents, the edges are social interactions.) Graphs of this kind are simply *networks*. A network is said to be *directed* if the interactions differ according to their direction taken among agents. This is expressed by an arrow which is attached to the edges. The number of connections among vertices is called *degree* of the network (or its *connectivity*). Connections which enter a vertex are counted by numbers which are called *in-degree*. Connections which leave a vertex are counted by numbers which are called *out-degree*. This is equivalent to the convention of speaking of "inputs" and "outputs" in terms of the processing of information. Graphs of such processes represent a process of computation. A directed network is very similar to a computer after all.

Such networks are also isomorphic to cellular automata. The latter are a sort of fundamental computer, one of the simplest types being the "game of life" introduced by Conway, a game that is able to simulate a simple form of evolution. If the number of vertices in a network remains constant, we speak of *equilibrium graphs*. If vertices vanish from or are added to the network such that we need a permanent updating, we speak of *non-equilibrium graphs*. (Typical examples of the latter are citation networks or networks of PhD students deriving from a given professor.)

If N is the number of vertices, L the number of edges and I the number of loops in the network, then it is always true that $I = L + 1 - N$. (This is a generalization of a theorem of Euler and gives for the hexagon, e.g., $I = 12 + 1 - 7 = 6$.) There is the *adjacency matrix* which is an $n \times n$ matrix, n being the number of vertices. If there are no loops, then all diagonal elements of this matrix are zero. The matrix is symmetrical, if the network is undirected. The degree of a vertex I is given by $k_i = \sum a_{ij}$, summing over all j for arbitrary indices. The total degree of the graph is $K = 2L$. The distribution of the degree can be given by $p(k, s, N)$ which is the probability that vertex s in a network of size N possesses exactly k connections. This vertex has k nearest neighbors in the network. The total distribution is $P(k, N) = 1/N \sum p(k, s, N)$ summing over all s from 1 to N. The first moment of the distribution (the average degree) is thus $\bar{k} = \sum k P(k)$ over all k. The total number of edges is $L = \frac{1}{2}\bar{k}N$.

Although we will not be dealing with stochastic situations here, it is nevertheless useful to list the most characteristic distributions which can be found in concrete cases. The most frequent distributions are of the Poisson type $P(k) = \exp(-\bar{k})\bar{k}^k/k!$ (which gives a curve in logarithmic coordinates similar to a parabola, with the maximum in the upper part), and the exponential distribution $P(k) \approx \exp(-k/\bar{k})$ (which gives a kind of semi-parabola). Important for evolutionary processes is the power law $P(k) \approx k^{-\gamma}$ with $k \neq 0$ and $\gamma > 1$ (which we call fractal). Networks of the latter type are said to be *scale-free*, because they cannot be oriented with respect of an average value. These networks are particularly important for processes of *percolation* which describe the most common type of transport of information in nature. One of the most well-known scale-free networks is the World Wide Web, with approximately 10^9 vertices.

The central problem of networks is the *clustering*. A vertex has z nearest neighbors such that maximal connectivity in the network is given, if all $\frac{1}{2}z(z + 1)$ possible vertices are present. If y is the total number of edges, then the *clustering* coefficient is given by $C = 2y/z(z - 1)$. In social networks one utilizes this phenomenon in order to discuss local groups which are densely networked (cliques). There, structure tells us something about the complexity and stability of networks. The important question in percolation theory is therefore, when do "gigantic connected components" of a network appear?

This is also related to *small worlds*, networks where the regular lattice structure is superposed by stochastic graphs. If m is the distance between a vertex and any of its mth nearest neighbors, then it is interesting to note the actual distribution of the numbers of these neighbors. Here $P(m, z)$ is the probability that a vertex of the network chosen at random possesses z m^{th} nearest neighbors. The distances between pairs of vertices are distributed according to the expected value of shortest paths, namely of the form $P(\lambda) = 1/N \sum z P_\lambda(z)$ over all z. In particular, one chooses here often a binomial distribution: $P_\lambda(z) := (N - 1 - z) P^z(\lambda)(1 - P(\lambda))^{N-1-z}$. Here λ is the shortest mean path.

Small worlds are known for the phenomenon that the inhabitants of the planet Earth form such a network, if the social interaction is simply "to know each other personally." One can prove that each person on Earth is connected to everybody else by means of maximally six connections, in terms of nearest neighbors of the sixth generation. The understanding of such networks is important for applications in the fields of internet research, epidemiology, stability research of networks, of neuronal networks, food chains and ecosystems.

We note the importance of games on directed graphs. We call them (referring to a famous novel of Hermann Hesse) *glass bead games*. They can be visualized as a model for determined computation. Clearly, each tree structure is a graph, and each tree game is the graph of a game. The division in proponent and opponent can be easily carried over to research games. In the language of categories, the morphisms of game categories are algorithms, pointing out the relationship to computation.

We can give two alternatives for a definition of games. According to Schleicher and Stoll, a game is a rooted tree with vertices which represent positions, and with directed edges which are called L and R (left/right). A game G is an ordered pair (L, R) which consists of two sets of games. Each game is the union of two self-games. This is an important aspect which shows up in the discussion of formalized hermeneutic in the sense of Jacques Lacan.

A more formal alternative is that of Trimble and Dolan. A game is a triple (X, r, f), where X is a set of positions, $r(X_0)$ is the initial position, and f is a mapping $f: X \to X$ such that to each $p \in X$ we associate the preceding position. Hence, $f(r) = r$. The *depth of position* p is then given by $f^n(p) = r$, $n \geq 0$. And p is *won* if it does not possess any continuations $f(p) = q$ with $(p! = r)$. The first player wins if the game has uneven depth and the second wins if it has even depth. A *winning strategy* for a game is a subset $S \subset X$ which is stable under f such that: 1. If p has even depth, then each continuation q of p is in S, and; 2. If p has uneven depth, then there is exactly one continuation q of p in S. Hence, winning strategies are subtrees of the game with root r.

Three additional remarks: A *holodeck game* of type T (as known from the *Star Trek* movie series) is a game whose positions are finite sequences which start with T and are defined by a recursion: 1. The initial position is the sequence of length 1, T; 2. If p is a position of even depth, then the continuation is cont(p): $T(2n)$, $T(m)$, and; 3. If p is a position of uneven depth, then cont(p): $T(2n)$, T', $T(m)$ T'.

All of the mentioned systems are constructive; that is, constructive parts of some actions f and g meet each other in order to generate $h = f(g)$. This operation can be visualized as the classical *modus ponens*: $f \wedge g \Rightarrow h$ in elementary (classical) logic. It is the "concentration" of f which determines its relevance. Utilizing this metaphor borrowed from chemistry gives us the possibility to speak of a "function gas." In mathematical terms this is simply the composition rule of functions.

We can add a topological description to the algebraical one when speaking of forms which are the results of the actions mentioned above. This is because the adjacency of some form β to another one α correlates with the probability for a transition from α to β: This is given by the fraction of the boundary which is common to neutral type sets (e.g., sets of genotypes) of β and α, respectively. And this fraction has to be compared with the total boundary of the neutral set of α. In other words, $S(\alpha)$ is the set of all sequences which fold α. And $\partial S(\alpha)$ is the boundary, i.e., the set of all sequences which are gained by one-point transitions of sequences in $S(\alpha)$. For any two α, β then, $S(\beta) \cap \partial S(\alpha)$ describes all those sequences which fold in β and are neighbors of those sequences that fold in α. The accessibility of β (as seen from α) is $A(\beta \cap \alpha) := |S(\beta) \cap \partial S(\alpha)| / |\partial S(\alpha)|$. It is this latter quantity which determines the evolution of states in nature.

****

Before coming back to these topics, we look at the systematic beginning of population dynamics. Because the concept of the latter stems from biology, we begin with biological populations which can consist of species which are in competition with each other in order to occupy territories which guarantee habitats and food sources for a given population. Competition can take various forms. *Mutualism* means that the development of one population depends on the development of another. *Host-Parasite relations* refer to the non-symmetrical situation in which one population has an advantage, the other a disadvantage. Populations of *predators* can be visualized as parasites of *prey* populations.

The important parameter which can describe the development of a population is the *growth rate R* of the population's density. If the population's density at a given time is x, and at another time x', then $x' = Rx$. The *updating* of generations leads after t generations to the value $R^t x$, where R is constant and larger than 1. In this case the population would explode into infinity after a while. This is the result of the differential equation $dx/dt = rx$ with the solution $x(t) = x(0) \exp(rt)$. (We note that the assumption of a continuous development is a considerable idealization of concrete situations.) Instead, in reality, growth is restricted very soon because a growing population can utilize smaller food reserves. (In social populations this depends on the strength of autonomous production by means of technologies.) In sufficiently linear terms the above equation is altered to $dx/dt = rx(1-x/K)$, with constants r and K. Obviously, the growth rate dx/dt is zero, if $x = 0$ (which is the trivial case), but also if $x = K$. For $0 < x < K$, growth takes place. For $x > K$, growth declines. Altogether the relevant solution of the generalized equation is:

$$x(t) = Kx(0)\exp(rt)/(K + x(0)(\exp(rt) - 1)).$$

We call K the environment's *carrier capacity* and classify the development as one of *logistic growth*.

In the discrete case, if y and y' are populations in two different generations, then $(y'-y)/y$ is the per capita rate of growth from one to the other generation. The evolution (difference) equations are similar to the above-mentioned differential equation, although the value of R has to be restricted to the interval between 0 and 4. We put then $x = y/K$ and $x' = y'/K$. Then we have $x' = F(x)$, with $F(x) := Rx(1-x)$. The relation displays a simple case of what we call *recurrence relations* which are of central importance for recent results in chaos theory. This equation, visualized as a mapping of the form $x \to Rx(1-x)$, defines a *dynamical system* in the mathematical sense. Here the point 0 is actually a fixed point. The orbit of x falls monotonously toward 0, if $R \leq 1$. For $R > 1$ the graph of F intersects the diagonal curve $y = x$ in one P whose abscissa defines another fixed point $p = R-1/R$. This fixed point is asymptotically stable, if $|dF/dx(p)| < 1$, and unstable in the other case.

In two generations x is being transformed into $F(F(x)) = F^{(2)}(x)$. We recognize from the above that $F^{(2)}$ is polynomial of degree 4 with a local minimum at ½ and two local maxima which are symmetrically to the left and to the right of ½. Again we have a fixed point P. For R between 1 and 3 (if p is asymptotically stable), this is the only point of intersection of that type. But for R between 3 and 4 we have to the left and to the right an additional point of intersection because the rise of the tangent at P is larger than 1. We call x *periodical point* of the dynamical system T, if there is some $k > 1$ such that $T^k x = x$. We call k *period*. Contrary to the continuous representation of the population model, the discrete case displays an intrinsic delay for one generation (due to the necessary updating of the system). This produces a permanent jumping back and forth of the system from one side of the fixed point to the other such that we have oscillations which will not settle down anymore. Indeed, $R = 3$ is what we call a *bifurcation* point, and for minimally smaller values p is essentially stable, while for minimally larger values periodic points show up that give instability. For R not much larger than 3 the points p_1 and p_2 are stable. But for even larger R they become unstable and further bifurcations appear. Above $R = 3.82$ all possible periods show up, and the structure of the orbits becomes considerably complicated. The system becomes more and more chaotic.

We learn from this that "computable" is not the same as "predictable" and that in the long run the determined motion cannot be differentiated from a motion at random. This insight with respect to concrete eco-systems goes back to a famous work of Robert May (1976).

The most prominent example for a dynamical system of the mentioned kind is the system of "Lotka-Volterra equations" which describe a prey-predator system modeling the shark behavior in the Adriatic sea after World War I. If x and y are the respective population densities, then the equations take the well-known form

$$\frac{dx}{dt} = x(a - by),$$

$$\frac{dy}{dt} = y(-c + dx).$$

There are three solutions: 1. $x(t) = y(t) = 0$; 2. $x(t) = 0$, $y(t) = y(0)\exp(-ct)$, and; 3. $y(t) = 0$, $x(t) = x(0)\exp(at)$. They are the trivial cases, and they represent three orbits: the origin which is a rest point, the positive y-axis, and the positive x-axis. These orbits form the boundary of a non-negative orthant $R^2(+) = \{(x,y) \in R^2: x \geq 0, y \geq 0\}$. This set is invariant in that all solutions that start in this set remain in it. In the interior of this region we have a rest point $F = (\xi, \eta)$ with $\xi = c/d$ and $\eta = a/b$. This point is surrounded by periodic orbits that run counterclockwise.

We can understand this in more precise terms. If we multiply the first line of the equations with $(c-dx)/x$ and the second with $(a-by)/y$, and add both of them, then we have the equation $(c/x-d)dx/dt + (a/y-b)dy/dt = 0$. This is actually the same as $d/dt\ (c\log x - dx + a\log y - by) = 0$. If we define then $H(x) := \xi\log x - x$, $G(y) := \eta\log y - y$, and also write $V(x, y) := dH(x) + bG(y)$, then we have $d/dt\ V(x(t), y(t)) = 0$, hence $V = $ const. So the function V remains constant along the orbits and is called *constant of motion*. We can interpret V as "altitude" of the point (x, y) within the relevant region of space. Then F would be the summit of this landscape. Solutions of the dynamic have to remain in regions of constant levels and return therefore to their starting point. The orbits are periodic. Depending on the initial conditions, the population densities of prey and predator will oscillate periodically with a given amplitude and frequency (wave length). Fishing reduces the rate of growth of predators. In the run of time the average density of predators declines and that of the prey is larger than in the case without fishing. An interval in fishing results in an increase of predators and a decline in the prey.

Of course, the equilibrium system of prey and predators is somewhat unrealistic, because in absence of the predator the prey would increase its density exponentially (see Hofbauer & Sigmund, 1998 for a detailed discussion. We follow here the general line of argument as put forward by these authors whose work is still quite paradigmatic for this topic). We have also to assume competition inside the population such that equations of the form:

$$\frac{dx}{dt} = x(a - ex - by),$$

$$\frac{dy}{dt} = y(-c + dx - fy),$$

with $e > 0$ and $f \geq 0$ would be much more realistic. Again, $R^2(+)$ remains invariant, and the boundary of the region consists of five orbits: the two rest points $(0, 0)$ and $P = (a/e, 0)$, the two intervals $]0, a/c[$ and $]a/c, \infty[$ on the x-axis and the positive y-axis. Further details can be discussed when we determine the *isoclines* (the x-isocline is given by the equation $ex + by = a$ and the y-isocline by $dx - fy = c$, namely for the case that the differentials vanish).

If $dx/dt = f(x)$ is a time-independent ordinary differential equation, and $x(t)$ is a solution which is defined for all $t \geq 0$ and fulfils the initial condition $x(0) = x$, then the ω-*limit* of x is the set of all cumulation points for $x(t)$ as $t \to \infty$, namely: $\omega(x) := \{y \in R^n, x(t_k) \to y, t_k \to \infty\}$. The points of this set have the property that all their neighborhoods are being visited by the solution $x(t)$. In particular, the set $\omega(x)$ is closed and invariant. Rest points and periodic orbits constitute their own ω-limits. If these are compact, they are also connected. And we can formulate (within the context of this present appendix we leave out all the proofs for theorems which can be found in the standard literature, especially in Hofbauer, 1998, mentioned above):

Theorem 1 (Lyapunov): Be $dx/dt = f(x)$ defined on a subset $G \subset R^n$. Be also the mapping $V: G \to R$ continuously differentiable. If there is a solution $x(t)$ for which the derivative dV/dt of the mapping $t \to V(x(t))$ fulfils the inequality $dV/dt \geq 0$, then $\omega(x) \cap G$ is contained in the set $\{x \in G: dV/dt = 0\}$.

In principle, by this theorem a motion is being described which follows the rise of a gradient. The existence of a Lyapunov function allows the validity of stability properties of ω-limits in that it characterizes a region of asymptotic stability, which remains constant within the vicinity of the minimum of the gradient. We have met such a function earlier, in the case of $V(x, y) = dH(x) + bG(y)$. The derivative in the theorem would be in that case $dV/dt = \partial V/\partial x \, dx/dt + \partial V/\partial y \, dy/dt$. If we remember the logarithmic representation of H and G, then we have:

$$d(\xi/x - 1)x(a - by - ex) + b(\eta/y - 1)y(-c + dx - fy).$$

Because ξ and η are actually solutions of isocline equations, we can replace a and c by $e\xi + b\eta$ and $d\xi - f\eta$, respectively, and get then $dV/dt = de(\xi - x)^2 + bf(\eta - y)^2 \geq 0$, such that we can apply the theorem of Lyapunov. The ω-limit for each orbit within region $R^2(+)$ is contained in the set $\{(x, y): dV/dt(x, y) = 0\}$. For $f > 0$ this set consists of the point F alone. For $f = 0$ it consists of the points $(x, y) \in R^2$, for which $y > 0$ and $x = \xi$. However, because the ω-limit must be again an invariant subset of this set, it reduces once more to F.

Again, the function $V(x, y)$ can be visualized as the "height" of a landscape at point (x, y). While the old solutions (of the equations without internal competition) follow the contour lines and remain on the same height, the new solutions (including competition) rise in height. The respective Lyapunov function describes a permanent "upward"-motion. This is illustrated by the gradient character of the motion. Stability (or asymptotic stability) characterizes a behavior of orbits which remain in the vicinity of critical points (in particular, of rest points) or even converge to these points. We speak of "attractors" and of their neighborhood as the "basin of attraction." Such stability situations indicate that each small perturbation which excites the system is compensated by a subsequent regulation performed by the system itself. If there is a rest point of type F, then stability is "larger" than in the case of the old system, while the old system changes simply from one periodical state to another, if perturbations act upon it. Even a small deviation of F will not alter the qualitative behavior of the system significantly, while in the old system the tiniest addition of competitional terms will radically change the system behavior. The former system is called *structurally stable*. Unfortunately, most systems in nature are non-linear such that their evaluation becomes extremely complicated and renders their solution practically impossible. Very often the method is approximative or qualitative by transforming the real system into a sufficiently linear system. This can be compared with the Taylor expansion of function as known from school mathematics. The structurally important things take place in the vicinity of the critical points of a system. Knowledge of these points is crucial for the understanding of the system. In fact, at critical points quantity turns into quality.

This is in fact a methodological advantage of the qualitative mathematics as originally introduced by Poincaré and developed further around 1975 by René Thom and Ilya Prigogine, leading forward to more recent theories of chaos, self-organized criticality and so forth.

We can generalize the above-mentioned results for systems with two (and more) species in competition. If the isoclines in a system of the last-discussed type for two species do not intersect in the interior of the relevant region, then one species will tend towards decay, while the other dominates. In case of an intersection $F = (\xi, \eta)$ we have to differentiate between two situations. Remember that $\xi = (af-cd)/(bf-ce)$ and $\eta = (bd-ae)/(bf-ce)$. If therefore $bf > ce$, then the denominators are positive, which means that $b/e > a/d > c/f$. We notice that each orbit in the interior of $R^2(+)$ converges to F. We call this case *stable coexistence*. If on the other hand, $c/f > a/d > b/e$, then all orbits of region II converge toward the y-axis, and all orbits of region IV converge toward the x-axis. F is a saddle point, and the two orbits which converge toward F must lie in the regions I and III. They divide this region into two basins of attraction. All orbits of one basin converge to $F_1 = (a/e, 0)$, the others to $F_2 = (0, d/f)$. Depending on the initial conditions, one or the other species will decay. This case is called *bistable*.

Systems of this type are said to be *cooperative*, if $\partial f_i/\partial x_j(x) \geq 0$ for all x. In that case the growth of each component is being enforced by the growth of any other component. Hence, we have:

Theorem 2: The Orbits of a two-dimensional cooperative system either converge to a rest point or tend toward infinity.

The same is true for a *competitive* system for which in the definition above ≥ has to be replaced by ≤.

One can also generalize the above results for the case of n populations that interact with each other such that the interactions are described by a suitable *interaction matrix* with components a_{ij}. Intensity, frequency, and quality of the interactions can be described then in more detail. Particularly interesting are the concrete situations of food chains in which one population is prey of another and predator of still another at the same time. In that case an explicit exclusion principle governs the occupation of ecological niches. If n populations depend on m resources such that $m < n$, then at least one population has to die out. But one soon realizes that, internally, the selection is not so strict. This is particularly obvious in the case of social animals for which competitive conflicts are being solved by *comment fights* of symbolical character. Power is represented by means of symbolically acting conventions rather than by a concrete fight resulting in the death of one individual. It was John Maynard Smith who first applied game theory to this apparently contradictory situation.

The simplest example of this is the case of two modes of behavior which govern the interaction in some population. One escalates the conflict until the opponent is injured or flees. The other conserves the symbolical state of representation and favors the retreat if the opponent escalates. Although linguistically not really correct, these two modes of behavior are traditionally referred to as *hawks* and *doves*. In evolutionary terms the outcome (gain) is the increase in fitness G, while an injury implies a loss of fitness C. The result of such a confrontation can be expressed in terms of a *pay off matrix*—of the simple form:

	If it encounters a hawk	If it encounters a dove
A hawk receives	½$(G-C)$	G
A dove receives	0	½G

Two doves receive (on the average) half the profit G, because either one or the other withdraws after a while. A dove which encounters a hawk withdraws and receives nothing, while the hawk remains with the full G. Two hawks will both escalate until one of them is incapacitated. The winner receives G, the loser C. On average, this is just half of the difference.

The inherent simplification is obvious. No state of information is being discussed about if the adversaries know whether the opponent is a hawk or a dove, or if it is a hawk pretending to be a dove or vice versa. But it is clear what the comment is all about. Costs of injury of hawks could actually reduce the numbers of hawks decisively. But comparatively harmless species such as doves are not really capable of avoiding escalation, once it takes place. This is why being a dove is much more complex than the example implies.

A behavior is said to be *evolutionarily stable* if, given the case that all members of the population do practice it, there is no dissident behavior which would overtake the population under the rules of selection.

Be then $W(I, Q)$ the fitness of an individuum of type I in a population of composition Q. Be also $xJ+(1-x)I$ that mixed population in which x means the frequency of the J-types and $1-x$ that of the I-types. Then a population of I-types will be evolutionary stable whenever a small amount of deviant J-types is being introduced, and the old I-type can thus produce always better results than the new type J.

$$W(J, \varepsilon J + (1-\varepsilon)I) < W(I, \varepsilon J + (1-\varepsilon)I)$$

for a small $\varepsilon > 0$. For a very small $\varepsilon \to 0$ we have $W(J, I) \le W(I, I)$ for all J. There is no type in a population of I-types which produces better results than the I-type itself. (The reverse is usually not true, because the second equation does not imply the equation above.) In the simple case of hawks and doves we do not find evolutionary stable behavior, because one can overtake the other. Only in the case that the situation is being escalated with a probability of $p = G/C$ can this behavior not be overtaken by someone else so that it is indeed evolutionary stable.

If we personalize somehow the populations or types (or individuals) as "players" who aim at a certain behavior, then we speak of *strategies*. The latter are either *pure* or *mixed,* according to whether they follow one of two alternatives (hawk or dove) or follow each possibility of behavior with a given probability. But the old pay off relations remain the same. Call the strategies p and q. Then the payoff for a p-strategist against a q-strategist is of the form:

$$p(Uq) = \Sigma_{ij} u_{ij} p_i q_j.$$

Here U is that matrix whose components are under the right hand side's sum. The indices run from 1 to N, where N is the number of available strategies. We call $\beta(q)$ the set of *best replies* to q, for which the mapping $p \to p(Uq)$ takes on a maximal value. We call that strategy which is the best reply to itself *Nash equilibrium.*

If we recall the types above, they are equivalent to different strategies, while the mixed form of the perturbation ansatz is the equivalent of a mixed strategy. A strategy p^* is called evolutionary stable, if for all p with $p \ne p^*$ the inequality $pU(\varepsilon p + (1-\varepsilon)p^*) < p^*U(\varepsilon p + (1-\varepsilon)p^*)$ is true. Ordering terms we notice that this condition is actually fulfilled, if we have equilibrium: $p(Up^*) \le p^*(Up^*)$ for all p—which is exactly the Nash equilibrium. But this is not quite sufficient, because there could be an alternatively best reply which overtakes p^*. Therefore, we also need the stability condition: if $p \neq p^*$ and $p(Up^*) = p^*(Up^*)$, then $p(Up)$ $< p^*(Up)$. (This last condition guarantees that p^* produces better results against p than p against itself.) Hence we have:

Theorem 3: Strategy p^* is evolutionary stable, iff $p^*(Uq) > q(Uq)$ for all $q \neq p^*$ in a neighborhood of p^*.

For the hawk-dove game, the strategy $p^* = (G/C, (C-G)/C)$ fulfills this condition and is thus evolutionary stable, because $p^*(Up)-p(Up) = 1/2C(G-Cp_1)^2$ is positive for all $p_1 \neq G/C$.

So far we have assumed that the success of a strategy depends essentially on the pairwise confrontation of opponents which are selected at random. But in reality, success depends on the average behavior of populations. Also, the concept of evolutionary stability assumes implicit dynamical aspects. Those can be modeled according to what we call *replicator equations*. Be a population divided into n types E_1 to E_n which show up with frequencies x_1 to x_n. Obviously, the fitness f of some type depends on the composition of the population which can be characterized by the state x (understood as vector). If the population is sufficiently large and the respective generations follow each other in a continuous fashion, then x can be visualized as continuously time-dependent. Then the growth rate of the form $(dx_i/dt)/x_i$ is the measure of the evolutionary success of one type in the population. In the sense of Darwin, we can understand this success as the difference between the fitness f of that type and the average fitness f of the whole population. We then have a replicator equation of the form:

$$dx_i/dt = x_i(f_i(x)-f(x)), \; i = 1 \ldots n.$$

If we admit mixed strategies (i.e., pure strategies R_i (here: i from 1 to N) which are being selected with a specific probability p_i, then a strategy is a point p in the simplex,

$$S_N = \{p = (p_1 \ldots p_N) \in R^N: p_i \geq 0, \Sigma p_i = 1\}.$$

With $a_{ij} := p^i U p^j$ for the payoff (expressed by means of some suitable $N \times N$-Matrix U) of an i-strategist against a j-opponent we have then as fitness of type i,

$$f_i(x) = \Sigma a_{ij} x_j = (Ax)_i,$$

where the sum runs over j. This is the replicator equation for the case of linear f_i. Here N (number of pure strategies) and n (number of types) are independent in the beginning. However, there is a parallel between points in S_N (strategies and $N \times N$-payoff) and points in S_n (players and $n \times n$-fitness) We can say that a point $x \in S_n$ is a symmetrical Nash equilibrium, if $xAx \leq xAx$ for all $x \in S_n$, and an evolutionary stable state, if $xAx > xAx$ for all $x \neq x$ in a neighborhood of x. We have also,

Theorem 4: 1. If $x \in S_n$ is a Nash equilibrium for a given game which is described by the payoff matrix A, then x is a rest point; 2. If x is the ω-limit of some orbit $x(t)$ in the interior of S_n, then x is a Nash equilibrium, and; 3. If x is Lyapunov stable,

116

then x is a Nash equilibrium.

Theorem 5: There is a differentiable and invertible mapping of S_n (i.e., of all x of S_n, which are positive) onto the positive part of the R^{n-1}, which also maps the orbits of the replicator equation onto the orbits of the Lotka-Volterra equation. (This means that properties of the one equation can be without loss of generality overtaken onto the other equation.)

Example: [Rock—Scissors—Paper] This game has three pure strategies (R_1 is beaten by R_2 which is beaten by R_3 which in turn is beaten by R_1). The payoff matrix can (if we normalize it such that the diagonal terms vanish) be written in the form:

$$A = \begin{pmatrix} 0 & -a_2 & b_3 \\ b_1 & 0 & -a_3 \\ -a_1 & b_2 & 0 \end{pmatrix}$$

where a, b, c are the three payoffs for proponent and opponent according to the three strategies. We find an interior rest point for this which is,

$$p = 1/k \ (b_2 b_3 + b_2 a_3 + a_3 a_2, \ b_3 b_1 + b_3 a_1 + a_1 a_3, \ b_1 b_2 + b_1 a_2 + a_1 a_2),$$

determined by three components in S_3.

Theorem 6: For the example we see that: 1. p is asymptotically stable; 2. p is globally stable; 3. $\det A > 0$, and; 4. $pAp > 0$.

If in particular the payoff matrix is symmetrical (thus $a_{ij} = a_{ji}$ for all i and j), the interests of the two players coincide. We call this a *partnership game*.

Theorem 7: For partnership games the average payoff xAx is a strict Lyapunov function. The asymptotically stable rest points of the associated replicator equation are the evolutionary stable states and given by the maxima of the average payoff. The asymptotically stable rest point in the interior of S_n is globally stable.

The *prisoners' dilemma* (pd) is a game for two players who have two options: to cooperate (C) or to defect (D). The payoff matrix takes the form:

$$\begin{pmatrix} R & S \\ T & P \end{pmatrix}$$

In other words, if both cooperate, they receive the reward R which is higher than the payoff P (punishment) they receive, if both of them defect. But if one of the players chooses D while the other chooses C, then the defecting receives payoff T (temptation) which is even higher than R while the cooperating receives only S (sucker's payoff) which is smaller than P. Also, it is assumed that $2R > T + S$, such that the total gain for both players is higher, if both cooperate rather than one cooperates and the other defects. (This is for avoiding that they can decide to alternate in that fashion and divide the gain afterward.) Obviously, it is strategy D that dominates the game. Two rational players will both defect and receive P which is smaller than R. If we think of a population of C-players and D-players, then the replicator dynamics makes sure that the cooperating will be extinguished. Nevertheless, in the economy as well as in biology, very often cooperation is actually being observed, particularly if the games are repeated very often. This is mainly because one has to take care of the tit-for-tat strategy, which is in fact the optimal strategy.

We can see this as follows. Take the case that there is a probability w for the taking place of the next round of the game. Then w^n is the probability that the n-th round takes place, and the sum over this ($= (1-w)^{-1}$) is the expected length of the game. If A_n is the payoff of the n-th round, then the total payoff is $A = \Sigma A_n w^n$.

We notice here the relationship between strategy and program or algorithm. A strategy for the repeated pd is simply a program which tells us what we have to do from round to round. Contrary to the game with one round only, the multitude of possible strategies now increases considerably. However, it is not quite possible to determine a best reply amidst all of this multitude. If the opponent plays *All-C*, then the proponent should play *All-D*. The total payoff is then $(1-w)^{-1}T$. If, however, the opponent plays *All-C* as long as the proponent is defecting for the first time and then switches to *All-D*, the best would be never to defect in order to not disturb the relationship. The gain of one round (T) is more than compensated by the following result, which is $(1-w)^{-1}P$. It can be shown by means of the famous Axelrod tournaments that the highest payoff is realized by a simple tit-for-tat strategy. (In fact, the generous variant of applying tit-for-tat after a repetition of defecting is apparently even more profitable in the long run.)

Frequently, players are not in symmetrical positions. They differ from each other with respect to the set of possible strategies. Asymmetric games in a pairwise fashion are called *bimatrix games*. Then we can look at the players in their respective positions I and II as is the case in chess. In position I, for the player n strategies are available; in position II, there are m strategies. Payoffs are given by matrices A and B. The player in position I utilizing strategy i against the player in position II utilizing strategy j has payoff a_{ij}, while his opponent has payoff b_{ij}. Mixed strategies for player I will be called $p \in S_n$, those for player II $q \in S_m$, and the respective payoffs are pAq and qBp.

Again, the pair $(p*, q*) \in S_n \times S_m$ is said to be the Nash equilibrium, if $p*$ is the best reply to $q*$ and $q*$ is the best reply to $p*$. Then $pAq* \leq p*Aq*$ for all p and $qBp* \leq q*Bp*$ for all q. The set of Nash equilibria for bimatrix games is always non-empty. For symmetric games we have $A = B$. A Nash equilibrium is said to be symmetric, if also $p = q$. (The latter can be asymmetric even in symmetric games, if the strategy of a hawk-dove game is to escalate when in position I and not to escalate when in position II.) For the asymmetric case we have two equations parallel to what we have mentioned above.

$$dx_i/dt = x_i((Ay)_i - xAy), \ i = 1 \ ... \ n,$$

$$dy_j/dt = y_j((Bx)_j - yBx), \ j = 1 \ ... \ m.$$

Let us take especially the case that $n = m = 2$. Then the associated matrices are:

$$\begin{pmatrix} 0 & a_{12} \\ a_{21} & 0 \end{pmatrix}, \begin{pmatrix} 0 & b_{12} \\ b_{21} & 0 \end{pmatrix}.$$

Because of $x_2 = 1-x_1$ and $y_2 = 1-y_1$, it suffices to consider x_1 and y_1 only, and we call them now simply x and y. Then we have the equations:

$$dx/dt = x(1-x)(a_{12} - (a_{12} + a_{21})y),$$

$$dy/dt = y(1-y)(b_{12} - (b_{12} + b_{21})x).$$

They are defined on the square $Q = \{(x, y) : 0 \le x, y \le 1\} \approx S_2 \times S_2$. If $a_{12}a_{21} \le 0$, then dx/dt does not change its sign in Q. One strategy of the two available for player I dominates the other. In this case x is either constant or converges monotonously toward 0 or 1. Similarly, $b_{12}b_{21} \le 0$. In the other case the equations possess a unique rest point in the interior of Q, namely,

$$F = (b_{12}/b_{12} + b_{21}, a_{12}/a_{12} + a_{21}).$$

The Jacobian matrix is,

$$\begin{pmatrix} 0 & -(a_{12} + a_{21})b_{12}b_{21}/(b_{12} + b_{21})^2 \\ -(b_{12} + b_{21})a_{12}a_{21}/(a_{12} + a_{21})^2 & 0 \end{pmatrix}$$

and the eigenvalues are $\pm \lambda$, where

$$\lambda^2 = a_{12}a_{21}b_{12}b_{21}/(a_{12} + a_{21})(b_{12} + b_{21}).$$

If $a_{12}b_{12} > 0$, then F is a saddle point and almost all orbits in the interior of Q converge to the one or the other corner of Q. If the reverse is true, then the eigenvalues are purely imaginary, and all orbits in the interior of Q are periodical orbits which circle around F.

The latter can be seen easily by dividing the right hand sides of the above equations by $xy(1-x)(1-y)$, which does not influence the orbits. We have then a Hamiltonian system of the form:

$$dx/dt = \partial H/\partial y, \ dy/dt = \partial H/\partial x,$$

where the Hamiltonian H is given by

$$H(x, y) = a_{12}\log y + a_{21}\log(1-y) - b_{12}\log x - b_{21}\log(1-x).$$

For our equations, H is a constant of motion, because dH/dt (after applying the chain rule twice) vanishes.

If we consider two types in a population which are in the state (p, q), then this state is probably not stable in the sense that if there is a state (x, y) which is in the vicinity of (p, q), then *not both types at the same time* could increase their payoff in going over into this state. Formally this means the following: We call a pair of strategies (p, q) *Nash-Pareto pair* for an asymmetric game with the payoff matrices A and B, if two conditions are fulfilled.

1. $pAq \geq xAq$ and $qBp \geq yBp$ for all (x, y)—equilibrium condition;

2. For all states (x, y) for which equality holds in the case of No. 1, we have: if $xAy > pAy \Rightarrow yBx < qBx$ and if $yBx > qBx \Rightarrow xAy < pAy$.

The first condition tells us that (p, q) is a pair in Nash equilibrium. The second tells us that it is impossible for both players at the same time to make an advantage out of going away from this equilibrium. At least one of them will be punished. (In classical game theory, this is equivalent to the concept of "Pareto optimality.") If the game is a *zero-sum game* then (p, q) is always a Nash-Pareto pair.

Well-known in biology is the equation for the *hypercycle,* introduced by Eigen and Schuster more than 20 years ago:

$$dx_i/dt = x_i(k_i x_{i-1} - \Sigma k_j x_j x_{j-1}),$$

where the sum is being taken over $j = 1 \dots n$ and the index i is being counted according to mod n. This equation is nothing but a replicator equation of the form $dx_i/dt = x_i((Ax)_i - xAx)$ on S_n, with a matrix A which is given by:

$$\begin{pmatrix} 0 & 0 & 0 & \cdots & \cdots & k_1 \\ k_2 & 0 & 0 & \cdots & \cdots & 0 \\ 0 & k_3 & 0 & \cdots & \cdots & 0 \\ 0 & 0 & k_4 & \cdots & \cdots & 0 \\ \vdots & \vdots & \vdots & \cdots & \cdots & \vdots \\ 0 & 0 & 0 & \cdots & k_n & 0 \end{pmatrix}$$

in the usual notation. Here, the x mean the relative frequencies of the RNA molecules which catalyze their mutual replication in a given feedback loop, which is visualized as a possible mechanism for the constructing of molecular carriers of information. The above equation possesses a unique rest point p in the interior of S_n, which is given by $k_1 x_n = k_2 x_1 = \dots = k_n x_{n-1}$ and $x_1 + x_2 + \dots + x_n = 1$. Then $p_i = (k_{i+1})^{-1} (\Sigma(k_{j+1})^{-1})^{-1}$ with $i = 1 \dots n$. (Sum over j.) If we change the coordinates and afterward the velocity (which is the same as performing a projective transformation of S_n onto itself), then we get rid of the k in the expressions and arrive at the above equation, if putting $k_1 = k_2 = \dots = k_n = 1$. The Jacobian is then the cyclic permutation matrix whose first line is $-2/n^2, -2/n^2, \dots, 1/n - 2/n^2$. The eigenvalues are $\gamma_0 = -1/n$ and otherwise for $j = 1 \dots n-1$: $\gamma_j = \Sigma(-2/n^2) \lambda^{kj} + 1/n \lambda^{(n-1)j} = \lambda^{-j}/n$ with $\lambda = e^{2\pi i/n}$. (Sum over k from 0 to $n-1$.) The rest point $m = 1/n$ I (indeed the eigenvalue γ_0 is associated with the eigenvector I which is orthogonal to the simplex S_n. For $n \geq 5$ it is unstable. The function $P(x) = x_1 x_2 \dots x_n$ vanishes on the boundary of S_n (on which $x_i = 0$ for at least one i), and is strictly positive in the interior. It has maximal value at point m.)

Theorem 8: For short hypercycles ($n = 2, 3, 4$) the interior rest point is globally stable.

However, for $n \geq 5$ it is unstable, and therefore we arrive at the question of whether a permanent coexistence of the various types of polynucleotides is possible at all. This is indeed the case, as can be seen from the following. The important point is not whether the chemical concentrations converge or oscillate, be it in a regular or irregular manner, but that they do not vanish. There must be a critical value $\delta > 0$ such that each solution of the equation in question fulfills the condition $x_i(t) > \delta$, for $i = 1 \dots n$, in the interior of the simplex, whenever t is sufficiently large. If from the beginning all species are present, even in only small quantities, then after a while there will still be a recognizable amount left of each of them. No perturbation which is smaller than δ would be able to extinguish molecular species. Dynamical systems which satisfy such a condition are called *permanent*. (Permanence implies more than just non-vanishing. The boundary of S_n acts as a repellor.) It can be shown that the hypercycle is permanent. The task is to give explicit criteria for the permanence of replicator equations of the type discussed.

Systems of the general type $dx/dt = x(f(x)-f)$ are said to be *permanent*, if there is a compact set K in the interior of the state space such that all orbits end in the interior of K. (The boundary is a repellor and points at infinity can be visualized as part of that boundary.) Also, permanence is a stronger criterion than *strong persistence*. Essentially, permanence means that there is a positive d such that $d < \lim \inf x_i(t)$, with t to infinity, for all i, whenever $x_i(0) > 0$ for all i. In the case of ecological equations we have additionally that there is some D such that also $\lim \sup x_i(t) \leq D$, with t to infinity, for all i, whenever $x \in \text{int } R^n(+)$. These conditions make sure that a species, if existing for the first time, will not be extinguished. For persistence, $\delta = 0$ suffices.

In most cases the f-terms can be written in a linear form such that we come back to a replicator equation of first order such as $dx/dt = x(Ax-xAx)$ or in the Lotka-Volterra form: $dx/dt = x(r + Ax)$. (The first version is defined on S_n while the second is defined on R^n. Again, we have suppressed indices here.)

Be U a subset of R^n and f a vector field on a neighborhood of the closure of U. A point $x \in U$ is called *regular*, if the determinant of the Jacobian of f is non-zero. A point $y \in R^n$ is called *regular value*, if for all $x \in U, f(x) = y$ is regular. As a consequence of the implicit function theorem, f is locally invertible in the vicinity of each such point x, and thus the roots of $f(x) = y$ are isolated. Moreover, the theorem of Sard states that almost each y is a regular value such that regular values are dense in R^n. Be now $y \notin f(\partial U)$. Then we define the *Brouwer degree* of f at y by: $\deg(f, y) := \Sigma \text{ sign det } Df$, if y is a regular value, and by: $\deg(f, y) := \lim \deg(f, y_n)$ otherwise. Here y_n is a sequence of regular values which converge to y. The degree counts the number of those roots of the equation $f(x) = y$, which conserve orientation, as well as the number of those which invert the orientation. (The sign of the determinant of the Jacobian is directly indicated here. Under the sum, the respective equation is usually written down: $f(x) = y$. The limit applies here for n to infinity.)

The crucial property of the degree is its *homotopy invariance*. If f_t ($t \in [0, 1]$) is a continuous family of mappings from the closure of U to the R^n, and if y does not belong to one of the values $f_t(\partial U)$, then $t \to \deg(f, y)$ is constant and also $\deg(f_1, y) = \deg(f_0, y)$ for all y. If then additionally y_0 and y_1 belong to the same component of $R^n \backslash f(\partial U)$ (if there is a continuous path $t \to y_t$ which does not intersect $f(\partial U)$ for $t \in [0, 1]$), then $\deg(f, y_0) = \deg(f, y_1)$.

Theorem 9: [Brouwer's fixpoint theorem] For each mapping h of the unit sphere $D = \{x \in R^n: \|x\| \leq 1\}$ to itself, there is some $x \in D$ such that $h(x) = x$.

Be now x^* an isolated rest point of the differential equation $dx/dt = f(x)$, defined on the open set $U \subseteq R^n$. Then we can define the *Poincaré index* of x^* with respect to f by:

$$i(x^*) := \deg(f, 0).$$

(Here f means the restriction onto a closed sphere $\mathrm{closure}(B) \subseteq U$, which contains x^*, but no other rest point.) If x^* is regular, then $i(x^*)$ is nothing but the sign of $\det Df$. Also: $i(x^*) = (-1)^s$, where s is the number of real negative eigenvalues of the Jacobian $D_{x^*}f$. The theorem of *Poincaré* and *Hopf* states that if f is a vector field on a compact manifold with boundary which points to the exterior as seen from the boundary points and possesses finitely many fixed points, then the relation $\Sigma i = \chi(M)$ is true. The sum is taken here over all rest points in M. The right hand side is what we call the *Euler characteristic*, a topological invariant on M which is important for concepts of harmony in geometry.

Theorem 10: If a system of ecological type is permanent, then the degree of the vector field is $(-1)^n$ with respect to each set U with $\mathrm{closure}(U) \subseteq \mathrm{int}\, R^n(+)$, which contains all interior ω-limits. In particular, there is a rest point in the interior of $R^n(+)$.

It is useful now to consider the following definition. A rest point p for a system of the ecological type is said to be *saturated*, if $f_i(p) \leq 0$ (or more generally $\underline{f_i}(p) \leq f(p)$), whenever $p_i = 0$.) Trivially, each rest point in the interior of the state space is saturated.

Theorem 11: There is at least one saturated rest point for general replicator systems. If all saturated rest points are regular, then the sum of their indices is just $(-1)^{n-1}$, and therefore their number is uneven.

For replicator equations of first order and for Lotka-Volterra equations the rest point p is saturated, if $(Ap)_i \leq pAp$ or, respectively, $r_i + (Ap)_i \leq 0$, whenever $p_i = 0$. This has the following important meaning:

The saturated rest points p of these equations are the (symmetrical) Nash equilibria for a game with the payoff matrix A:

122

$$xAp \leq pAp \text{ for all } x \in S_n.$$

The existence of Nash equilibria and the result on their uneven number, if they are regular, are immediate corollaries of theorem 11. It is such that the evolution equations for populations of ecosystems are directly related to the concrete criteria of game theory. Another important consequence is:

Theorem 12: A replicator system is permanent if there is some $p \in$ int S_n such that the relation $pAx > xAx$ is true for all rest points $x \in \partial S_n$.

In order to prove permanence, we have to check whether there is a positive solution p for the linear inequalities $\Sigma p_i((Ax)_i - xAx) > 0$, where the sum runs over those i for which $x_i = 0$. (And for which x runs through the rest points on the boundary.) The set of solutions p shows up as an open convex subset of the interior of S_n.

We can generalize the results mentioned here to replicator networks, in particular to catalytic networks. Because of the increasing complexity of the representations involved, it is helpful that there is a relationship between the permanence of a system and the irreducibility of its directed graph, which facilitates the analysis. We can see that if $dx_i/dt = x_i((Ax)_i - xAx)$ is permanent with $a_{ij} \geq 0$, then the graph of the system is irreducible. (A directed graph is said to be *irreducible* if there is for any two corners i and j an oriented path from i to j.)

Remember now that all higher organisms in biology contain a genetic program which is saved in the chromosomes. The number of the chromosomes varies depending on the species, but they always show up in homologous pairs. If a diploid cell of this kind divides, then each chromosome is being duplicated, and the two daughter cells each contain a complete set of chromosomes. (In the case of human beings there are also haploid cells which contain only half of the chromosomes, one of each pair. These are the germ cells.) A genetic property which is manifested in the phenotype is in the simplest case determined by the mutual action of two genes which sit in their positions on a pair of homologous chromosomes. Positions (loci) can be occupied by different gene types which are called *alleles*.

Be the probabilities for the respective alleles $A_1 \ldots A_n$ given by $x_1 \ldots x_n$ and those for the gene pairs (A_i, A_j) by x_{ij} with $1 \leq i, j \leq n$. A gene chosen at random sits with probability $\frac{1}{2}$ on the "first position" (transmitted by the father) and with probability $\frac{1}{2}$ on the "second position." In the first case it is of type A_i, if the pair is of form (A_i, A_j). In the second case it is of this type, if the pair has the inverted form. Hence, we have,

$$x_i = \frac{1}{2}\Sigma x_{ij} + \frac{1}{2}\Sigma x_{ji},$$

the sum over the j. Be x' the probabilities for the next generation. Under random conditions we have then $x'_{ij} = x_i x_j$. And thus:

$$x'_i = x_i.$$

This result implies the *Hardy-Weinberg law*: 1. The probabilities for the genes remain invariant from generation to generation. 2. From the first daughter generation onward, the probabilities for homocygotic genotypes A_iA_j are given by x_j^2, for heterocygotic genotypes by $2x_ix_j$.

Usually, gene pairs have to be differentiated according to with what probability w_{ij} they reach maturity. The selective values fulfill the conditions $w_{ij} \geq 0$ and $w_{ij} = w_{ji}$. If N is the number of cygotes in the new generation, then Nx_ix_j of them carry the gene pair (A_i, A_j), and $w_{ij}Nx_ix_j$ of them survive until maturity. The total number of individuals which reach the state of next pairing is equal to the sum over the last expression summed from 1 to n. We call x'_{ij} *frequency of the gene pair* (A_i, A_j) in the new generation in state of maturity, and x'_i *frequency of allele* A_i, and have then:

$$x'_{ij} = w_{ij}Nx_ix_j / \Sigma w_{rs}Nx_rx_s,$$

where the summing is over r and s (from 1 to n). With the above-mentionend relation for x_i and bearing the symmetry of w in mind, we get then also:

$$x'_i = x_i(\Sigma w_{ij}x_j / \Sigma w_{rs}x_rx_s),$$

which describes the evolution of the gene frequencies from one to the next generation.

Theorem 13: In a system which satisfies the last-mentioned equation, alternatively written as $x'_i = x_i (Wx)_i / xWx$, the *average fitness* $w(x) = xWx$ increases along each orbit, in the sense that $w(x') \geq w(x)$, where equality is valid iff x is a rest point.

The consequences of this result point to the fact that in the case of mutations, their recurrence, which is directed onto one allele, leads to a conservation of that allele, even when selection threatens with extinction. This is the important meaning of mutations for the gene pool. (This is particularly surprising because mutations are nothing but duplication errors in the first place. Errors have an important function of redundance.)

There is still the other possibility, describing the number of alleles as variable of time, provided the population is sufficiently large and birth and death cases happen in a roughly continuous manner. If the total number of individuals is N, then $2N$ is the total number of the genes and $N_i/2N$ is the relative frequency for the allele A_i. Let us assume that the population is in an Hardy-Weinberg equilibrium at any time. Then the frequency of the gene pair (A_i, A_j) is given by $x_ix_j = (4N^2)^{-1}N_iN_j$. Let d be the death rate and b the birth rate (with indices ij). Then $m = b-d$ is called *Malthusian fitness*. (Let us also assume the latter's constancy.) This parameter is symmetric in the indices. For the growth of the allele A_i within the given gene pool can be described by:

$$dN_i/dt = N_i/2N \ \Sigma m_{ij}N_j,$$

the sum over the j. For the relative frequencies we have (written in matrix fashion),

$$\mathrm{d}x_i/\mathrm{d}t = x_i((Mx)_i - xMx).$$

This equation is called *selection equation* of population genetics. (We know from earlier discussion that the asymptotically stable rest points of this equation are nothing but the evolutionary stable strategies of the game which is defined in terms of the matrix M. The average fitness $m(t) = x(t)Mx(t)$ is a strict Lyapunov function of this equation.)

Theorem 14: Each orbit of the selection equation converges to a rest point.

Game theory can be visualized as an instrument which can be used to study frequency-dependent selection. The idea is that the microscopic genotypes imply strategies which are actually manifested in the macroscopic behavior of the phenotypes.

Let us briefly come back to partnership games (Theorem 7). We have seen that for these games the matrix A is symmetrical and that the average payoff xAx is a strict Lyapunov function. From theorem 1 we know that such functions are always related to specific derivatives. In that case, this can be described by means of a function $V(x) = xAx$ which is of the form $\mathrm{d}V(x)/\mathrm{d}t = 2\Sigma x_i((Ax)_i - xAx)^2 \geq 0$. In the case of partnership games the average payoff is not only a Lyapunov function but even a potential for the underlying equation, as we can see from the last section (replacing M by a general A). Then, let us suppose that M is a manifold and G a Riemannian metric with components $g_{ij}(x)$. Let $V(x)$ also be a differentiable function on M with values in R. Then the derivative $DV(x)$ is a linear mapping from the tangent space at x to R. Therefore, there is a vector v in tangent space such that it equals the derivative. We call this the *G-gradient of V at x*. The vector field $\mathrm{d}x/\mathrm{d}t = v(x)$ defines then a dynamical system, and V is said to be its potential. The relation to the classical gradient is in the fact that if M is an open subset of R^n, then the G-gradient of V is given by $1/G(x)\nabla V(x)$.

If $g_{ij}(x) = 1/x_i\delta_{ij}$, the metric is called *Shahshahani metric*. The replicator equation discussed above is in the case of a symmetrical matrix V nothing but a Shahshahani gradient whose potential is one half of the average payoff: $V(x) = \frac{1}{2}xAx$. If $\mathrm{d}x_i/\mathrm{d}t = f_i(x) = \partial V/\partial x_i$ is a classical (Euclidean) gradient vector field on the R^n, then the associated replicator equation $\mathrm{d}x_i/\mathrm{d}t = x_i(f_i(x) - f(x))$ is a Shahshahani gradient on the interior of S_n with the same potential function V. For a vector field which is defined in that manner, in some neighborhood U of the interior of S_n, the following conditions are equivalent: 1. The right hand side is a Shahshahani gradient; 2. There are functions $V, G: U \to R$, such that $f_i(x) = \partial V/\partial x_i + G(x)$ on the interior of S_n; 3. The Jacobian is symmetrical for each x, and; 4. The relationship $\partial f_i/\partial x_j + \partial f_j/\partial x_k + \partial f_k/\partial x_i = \partial f_j/\partial x_k + \partial f_i/\partial x_j + \partial f_k/\partial x_j$ is true on the interior of S_n for all i, j, k. (The last condition is also called *triangular integrability condition*.)

Consider now a game with N pure strategies R_i, where the payoff F_i depends on the average frequencies of the strategies p_i only. Assume that the gene pool contains alleles A_1 bis A_n with frequencies x_1 to x_n such that the frequency of the gene pair (A_i, A_j) is given by $x_i x_j$ according to the Hardy-Weinberg law and that such a gene pair gives the phenotype $p(ij) \in S_N$. Then the average mixture of strategies p in the population is given by $p(x) = \Sigma p(ij) x_i x_j$. (Sum over the i, j.) The frequency of strategies which are "played" by allele A_i is,

$$p^i(x) = \Sigma p(ij) x_j = \tfrac{1}{2} \partial p / \partial x_i,$$

sum over the j only. The frequency-dependent payoff for individuals of type (A_i, A_j) is $w_{ij} = p(ij) F(p)$. The average payoff for allele A_i is thus $f_i(x) = p^i F(p)$. The evolution of the gene pool satisfies the selection equation of the form:

$$dx_i / dt = x_i (p^i - p) F(p) = x_i (f_i(x) - f),$$

which is obviously a replicator equation. At the same time, this is also a "strategy equation" for pure strategies. Hence, we have the following.

Theorem 15: If the equation for pure strategies is a Shahshahani gradient with potential $V(y)$, then also the frequency-dependent selection equation is such a gradient with potential $\tfrac{1}{2} V(p(x))$.

This theorem represents the relationship between game theory and selection theory. We can translate the result such that the strategy of the population tries to approximate an evolutionary stable strategy as close as possible according to the given constraints. The point is that subsequently, mutants can only enter the population if their mere existence allows for the others to approximate the evolutionary stable strategy even better. If the population has actually reached that strategy once, then only such mutants can enter which do not alter the average strategy of the population.

****

So what we have seen is essentially the following. Each form of behavior manifests itself by means of a game of trial and error. Such a stepwise adaptation to the environment can be achieved either by individual learning or selection. According to the important works of Maynard Smith, processes of this kind can be suitably modeled in terms of game theory. Contrary to classical game theory, which is mainly based on statistics, evolutionary game theory is based on a dynamical description which replaces the concept of rational players by the population dynamics of behavioral programs. We have seen in the preceding how a non-linear dynamical description of self-organizing processes can be given. We analyze the question of why replicator equations, which demonstrate how successful strategies are propagated through populations, create new conditions while at the same time questioning their own success. Such considerations are obviously at the root of those results which may show under which explicit conditions conflicts can escalate in evolutionary games of this type, how equilibria can eventually emerge and what cooperation can actually mean.

In some ecosystems there is the macro-level of phenotypes, which are the *observable* forms which express qualities of the system. The latter are themselves the result of a network of interactions which unfold their actions in the space of the system. Interactions among phenotypes—mediated by individuals—are types of behavior. It is in this behavior where the triad of cognition, communication, and cooperation important for systems manifests itself in detail. These concepts can be carried over to other domains of phenomena such as the physical domain, the chemical domain, the biological one and the social one. Although we have to carefully define the spaces, networks and levels of interactions each time we talk about one of these domains, the essential form of mediation among these spaces, networks and levels does not structurally change at all.

On the micro-level, there is a similar network of interactions governing the behavior of genotypes, with their own systematic space. On the macro-level as well as on the micro-level the vertices of the networks represent the agents of the processes taking place, and the edges represent the directed interactions among them. These *unobservable* actions on the micro-level produce the *observable* actions on the macro-level such that the latter are *emergent* with respect to the former. By modeling the systems involved, one has to start in a top-down fashion, beginning with what is observable and going down onto the level which is not.

In the language of mathematical categories, the objects on the macro-level are the forms or phenotypes themselves while the morphisms are the interactions. Accordingly, on the micro-level the objects are the genotypes and the morphisms are the interactions. Equivalently, interactions can be described in terms of operations, or alternatively, in terms of strategies. The optimization of the latter can be described in terms of the network properties as to shortest distances among vertices, the formation of clusters (cliques) or even small-world theories. The process of emergence itself can be expressed in terms of a functor, which maps the respective categories onto each other.

References

Albiac, G. (1997). "The Empty Synagogue", in W. Montag and T. Stolze (eds.), *The New Spinoza*, ISBN 91440816625417 pp. 109-144.

Arshinov, V. and C. Fuchs (eds.) (2003). *Causality, Emergence, Self-Organization* (INTAS Volume 1), Russian Academy of Science, NIA-Priroda, Moscow. No ISBN

Asthekar, A., Baez, J. C. and Krasnov, I. (2000). "Quantum Geometry of Isolated Horizons and Black Hole Entropy," www.arXiv.org/pdf/gr-qc/0005126 .

Atlan, H. (1998). "Immanent Causality. A Spinozist Viewpoint on Evolution and Theory of Action," in: G. Van de Vijver, S. N.Salthe and M. Delpos, (eds.), *Evolutionary Systems. Biological and Epistemological Perspectives on Selection and Self-Organization*, ISBN 0-7923-5260-2, pp. 215-231.

Baez, J. C. and Stay, M. (2008). "Physics, Topology, Logic, and Computation: A Rosetta Stone," http://math.ucr.edu/home/baez .

Balibar, E. (1997). Ius – Pactum – Lex. On the Constitution of the Subject in the Theologico-Political Tractate. In: W. Montag and T. Stolze (eds.), *The New Spinoza*, ISBN 109-144 0816625417, pp. 171-205.

Barbieri, M. (2003). *The Organic Codes. An Introduction to Semantic Biology*, ISBN 0-521-82414-1.

Bartuschat, W. (1992). *Spinozas Theorie des Menschen*, ISBN 3-7873-1090-8.

Bayertz, K. (ed.) (1993). *Evolution und Ethik*, ISBN 3-15-008857-7.

Benjamin, W. (1982). *Das Passagen-Werk*. ISBN 3-518-11200-7.

Benjamin, W. (1970). *Berliner Chronik*. ISBN 3-518-01251-7.

Bennett, J. (1996). "Spinoza's Metaphysics," in: D. Garrett (ed.), *The Cambridge Companion to Spinoza*, ISBN 9780521398657, pp. 61-88.

Beretta, G. P. (2008). "Quantum Thermodynamics. Microscopic Foundations of Entropy and of Entropy Generation by Irreversibility," *Atti dell'Accademia Peloritana dei Pericolanti*, *LXXXVI*, ISBN 978-0-486-43932-7, pp. 1-22.

Bergmann, L., Schaefer, C. and Gobrecht, H. (1970). *Lehrbuch der Experimentalphysik*, ISBN 3-11-002091-2 (see in particular vol. 1, 678.).

Blass, Andreas (1988). "Topoi & Computation," (reprint from the website) http://www. math.lsa.umich.edu/~ablass/comp.html .

Bell, J. L. (1988). *Toposes and Local Set Theories*, ISBN 0-19-853274-1.

Bloch, E. (1985). *Spuren*, ISBN 3-518-28150-X.

Bloch, E. (1982). *Das Prinzip Hoffnung*, ISBN 3-518-00942-7.

Boi, L. (2005a). "Topological Knot Models in Physics and Biology," in: L. Boi (ed.), *Geometries of Nature, Living Systems, and Human Cognition. World Scientific*, ISBN 9812564748, pp. 203-278.

Boi, L. (ed.) (2005b). *Geometries of Nature, Living Systems, and Human Cognition. World Scientific*, ISBN 9812564748.

Boje, D. (2004). "How von Bertalanffy's Critique of Marxist System Theory Self-Deconstructs," (From the website New Mexico State University) peace@peaceaware.com: See http://cbae.nmsu.edu/~dboje/).

Bounias, M., and Bonaly, A. (2000). "The Future of Life on Earth: Ecosystems as Topological Spaces," in: V. Burdyuzha, G. Khozin (eds.), *The Future of the Universe and the Future of Our Civilization*. ISBN 981-02-4264-6, pp. 206-244.

Bounias, M. (1990). *La Création de la vie: de la matière à l'esprit*, ISBN 2-26800-872-X.

Bourdieu, P. (1982). *Die feinen Unterschiede*, ISBN 3-518-57625-9.

Boyd, J. P. (1979/80). "The Universal Semigroup of Relations," *Social Networks 2*, ISSN 0378-8733, pp. 91-117.

Boyd, J. P. and Everett, M. G. (1999). "Relations, residuals, regular interiors, and relative regular equivalence," *Social Networks 21*, ISSN 0378-8733, pp. 147-165.

Carbone, A. (2005). "Pathways of Deduction," in: L. Boi (ed.), *Geometries of Nature, Living Systems, and Human Cognition. World Scientific*, ISBN 9812564748, pp. 383-399.

Crutchfield, J. P. (1994). *The Calculi of Emergence. Physica D (special issue on complex systems)*. (Also available as SFI 94-03-016 at the Sante Fe institute.) ISSN 0167-2789.

Curley, E. (1988). *Behind the Geometrical Method. A Reading of Spinoza's Ethics*, ISBN 978-0691020372.

Dekker, A. H. (2007). "Studying organisational Topology with Simple Computational Models," *JASSS 10 (46)*, ISSN 1460-7425, pp. 1-11.

Dekker, A. H. (2001). "A Category-Theoretic Approach to Social Network Analysis," *E-Notes in Theor. Comp. Sci. 61*, ISSN 1073-0486, pp. 1-13.

Deleuze, G. (1997). Spinoza and the Three "Ethics". In: W. Montag and T. Stolze (eds.), *The New Spinoza*, ISBN 109-144 0816625417, pp. 21-34.

Deleuze, G. (1968). *Spinoza et le problème de l'expression*, ISBN 2-7073-0007-1.

Dobronravova, I. and Hofkirchner, W. (eds.) (2004). "Science of Self-Organization and Self-Organization of Science," *INTAS Volume 2*, ISBN 3-89958-107-5.

Edmonds, B. (1999). *Syntactic Measures of Complexity*. PhD thesis. University of Manchester. Philosophy Dept.

Engels, F. (1845). *Die Lage der arbeitenden Klasse in England*, MEW 2, ISBN 3-320-00611-8, pp. 225-506.

Floridi, L. (2004)."Information," in: L. Floridi (ed.), *The Blackwell Guide to the Philosophy of Computing and Information*, ISBN 0631229183, pp. 40-61.

Fontana, W. (1991). "Algorithmic Chemistry," in: C.G.Langton (ed.), *Artificial Life II*, ISBN 0201525712.

Freeman, L. C. (1996). "Cliques, Galois lattices, and the structure of human social groups", *Social Networks 18*, ISSN 0378-8733, pp. 173-187.

Freidel, L. and Krasnov, K. (1999). "Simple Spin Networks as Feynman Graphs," www.arXiv.org/pdf/hep-th/9903192 .

Freud, S. (1986). *Letters to Wilhelm Fliess (1887-1904)*, ISBN 3-10-022802-2.

Freud, S. (1982). *Studienausgabe der Werke, Band 3*, ISBN 3-596-27303-X.

Freyd, P. J. and Scedrov, A. (1990). *Categories, Allegories*, ISBN 0444703675.

Frohnhofen, A. (2001). *Raum – Region – Ort. Sozialraeume. Perspektiven Jugendlicher*, Dissertation. ISBN 3-8100-3603-X.

Fuchs, C. and Zimmermann, R. E. (2008). "Practical Civil Virtues in Cyberspace. Towards the Utopian Identity of civitas and multitudo," in *Muenchener Schriften zur Design Science*, Band 5 [In press] .

Funke, J. and Wassmann, J. (1999/2000). "Raum und Zeit aus psychologischer Sicht", Hauptseminar. www.psychologie.uni-heidelberg.de/AE/allg/lehre/ethn/ws99_rz_plan.htm .

Gabbey, A. (1996). "Spinoza's natural science and methodology," in: D. Garrett (ed.), *The Cambridge Companion to Spinoza*, ISBN 0521398657, pp. 142-191.

Garret, D. (ed.) (1996). *The Cambridge Companion to Spinoza*, ISBN 0521398657.

Garrett, D. (1996). "Spinoza's ethical theory," in: D. Garrett (ed.), *The Cambridge Companion to Spinoza*, ISBN 0521398657, pp. 267-314.

George, E. (2006). *What Came Before He Shot Her*, ISBN 9780340827505.

Girard, J.-Y. (2003). *Locus Solum. From the rules of logic to the logic of rules*,ISSN 0960-1295.

Girard, J.-Y. (1989). *Proofs and Types*, ISBN 0521371813.

Goldblatt, R. (1984). *Topoi. The Categorial Analysis of Logic*, ISBN 0486450260.

Hardt, M. and Negri, A. (2004). *Multitude. War and Democracy in the Age of Empire.* ISBN 1-594-20024-6.

Hardt, M. and Negri, A. (2000). *Empire*, ISBN 0-674-00671-2.

Henriques, G. (1992). "Morphisms and Transformations in the Construction of Invariants," in: J. Piaget et al., *Morphisms and Categories. Comparing and Transforming*, ISBN 0-8058-0300-9, pp.183-206 (ch. 13).

Hesse, H. (1977). *Das Glasperlenspiel.* ISBN 3518365797.

Hodges, W. (1997). *A shorter model theory*, ISBN 0-521-58713-1.

Hofbauer, J. and Sigmund, K. (1998). *Evolutionary Games and Population Dynamics*, ISBN 0-521-62570-X.

Hofkirchner, W. et al. (2007). "ICTs and Society. The Salzburg Approach," in *ict&s centre research paper series no. 3,* http://icts.sbg.ac.at/media/pdf/pdf1490.pdf .

Houston, R. (2003). *Categories of Games,* Master thesis, University of Manchester. No ISBN.

Johnstone, P.T. (1977). *Topos Theory*, ISBN 0-12-387850-0.

Johnstone, P.T. (2002-2003). *Sketches of an Elephant: A Topos Theory Compendium*, 2 vols, ISBN 019852496X.

Juranville, A. (1990). *Lacan und die Philosophie*, (PUF 1984), ISBN 3-924963-05-3.

Kappraff, J. (2001). *Connections. The Geometric Bridge Between Art and Science.* ISBN 981-02-4585-8.

Karpov, E., Ordonez, G., Petrosky, T. and Prigogine, I. (2003). "Microscopic Entropy and Nonlocality," in *Particles & Nuclei Letters 1 (116)*, ISSN 0094-243X, pp. 8-15.

Kauffman, L. H. (2005). BKnots," in L. Boi, (ed.), *Geometries of Nature, Living Systems, and Human Cognition.* ISBN 9812564748, pp. 131-202.

Kauffman, L. H. (2002). "Biologic," www.arXiv.org/pdf/quant-ph/0204007.

Kauffman, L. H. (2001). "Quantum Computing and the Jones Polynomial," www.arXiv. org/pdf/math.QA/0105255 .

Kauffman, L. H. (1995). "Knot Logic," in: L. H. Kauffman (ed.), *Knots and Applications*, ISBN 9810220049, pp. 1-110.

Kauffman, L. H. (1993). *Knots and Physics.* [Here according to the German edition], ISBN 3-86025-232-1.

Kauffman, S. (2000). *Investigations. The Nature of Autonomous Agents and the Worlds They Mutually Create*, ISBN 019512104X.

Kitcher, P. (1992). *Freud's Dream. A Complete Interdisciplinary Science of Mind*, ISBN

0-262-61115-5.

Klever, W. N. A. (1996). "Spinoza's life and works," in: D. Garrett (ed.), *The Cambridge Companion to Spinoza*, ISBN 0521398657, pp. 13-60.

Knodt, R. (2006). "Mariposa," www.reinhardt-knodt.de/text_mariposa.html.

Kouznetsov, B. (1967). "Spinoza and Einstein," *Revue de synthèse 88*, ISSN 0035-1776 pp. 45-46; fasc. 3, pp. 31-52.

Lambek, J., P. and Scott, J. (1986). *Introduction to Higher Order Categorical Logic*, ISBN 0521246652.

Lawvere, F. W. (1963, 1968). *Functorial Semantics of Algebraic Theories and Some Algebraic Problems in the Context of Functorial Semantics of Algebraic Theorie,* PhD thesis. Columbia University, New York.

Lawvere, F. W. and Rosebrugh, R. (2003). *Sets for Mathematics*, ISBN 0521804442.

Lefebvre, H. (1991). *The Production of Space*, ISBN 0631140484.

Lévi-Strauss, C. (1949). *Les structures élémentaires de la parenté.* (English version: Beacon, Boston, 1969.) ISBN 0807046698.

Lewin, K. (1934). "Der Richtungsbegriff in der Psychologie," *Psych. Forsch. XIX*, ISSN 0340-0727, pp. 249-299.

Lewin, K. (1936). *Principles of Topological Psychology*, ISBN 978-0384324602.

Leyton, M. (2001). *A Generative Theory of Shape*, ISBN 3-540-42717-1.

Lloyd, G. (1994). *Part of Nature. Self-Knowledge in Spinoza's Ethics*, ISSN 0031-8108.

Loeb, A. L. (1993). *Concepts & Images. Visual Mathematics*, ISBN 0-8176-3620-X.

Loh, W., Mall, R. A. and Zimmermann, R.E. (2008). *Interkulturelle Logik.*

Lorenzer, A. (1970). *Sprachzerstoerung und Rekonstruktion*, ISBN 3518076310.

Lorenzer, A. (1977). *Sprachspiel und Interaktionsformen*, ISBN 3-518-07681-7.

MacLane, S. (1971). *Categories for the Working Mathematician*, ISBN 3-540-90036-5.

MacLane, S. and Moerdijk. I. (1992). *Sheaves in Geometry and Logic: A First Introduction to Topos Theory*, ISBN 0387977104.

Majima, H and Suzuki, A. (2005). "The Role of Interaction in Open Quantum Systems and the Second Law of Thermodynamics," *J. Korean Phys. Soc. 46 (3)*, ISSN 0374-4884, pp. 678-683.

Martin, J. (2003). "Comment on ch. 2 of von Bertalanffy's General Systems Theory. T554 discussions," http://systems.open.ac.uk/page.cfm?pageid=resourceBert.

May, R. (1976). "Simple mathematical models with very complicated dynamics," *Nature 261*, ISSN 0028-0836, pp. 459-467.

Mazzola, G. (2008). *Jazz and the Creative Flow of Collaborative Gestures*, http://www.uni-duisburg-essen.de/ekfg/forschung/ekfg_49816.shtml.

Mazzola, G. (2002). *The Topos of Music. Geometric Logic of Concepts, Theory, and Performance*, ISBN 0817657312.

Mazzola, G. (1997). "Topologien gestalteter Motive in Kompositionen," (reprint from the website) http://www.uni-koeln.de/phil-fak/muwi/fricke/145mazzola.pdf .

Mazzola, G. (1995). "Towards Big Science: Geometric Logic of Music and its Technolog," (reprint from the website), http://citeseerx.ist.psu.edu/viewdoc/summary?doi=10.1.1.51.4832 .

Montag, W. and Stolze, T. (eds.) (1977). *The New Spinoza*, ISBN 978-0816625406.

Morin, E. (1977). *La méthode. 1. La Nature de la Nature*. ISBN 2020058197.

Negri, A. (1997). "Reliqua Desiderantur: A Conjecture for a Definition of the Concept of Democracy in the Final Spinoza," in: W. Montag, T. Stolze (eds.), *The New Spinoza*, ISBN 978-0816625406, pp. 218-246.

Negri, A. (1991). *The Savage Anomaly*, ISBN 0816618763.

Neuman, Y. and Nave, O. (2007). *A Mathematical Theory of Sign-Mediated Concept Formation*, ISSN 0096-3003.

Noll, T. (2005). "The Topos of Triads," in: H. Fripertinger, L. Reich (eds.), *Colloquium on Mathematical Music Theory, Grazer Mathematische Berichte 347*, ISSN 1016-7692, pp. 1-26.

Norris, C. (1991). *Spinoza and the Origins of Modern Critical Theory*, ISBN 0631175571.

Paty, M. (1986). "Einstein and Spinoza," in: M. Grene, D. Nails (eds.), *Spinoza and the Sciences*, ISBN 90-277-1976-4, pp. 267-302.

Piaget, J., Henriques, G. and Ascher, E. (1992). *Morphisms and Categories. Comparing and Transforming*, ISBN 0-8058-0300-9.

Pietarinen, J. (2002). "Comments to Zimmermann's Spinoza Paper," in: E. Martikainen (ed.), *Infinity, Causality, and Determinism*, ISBN 3-631-39146-3, pp. 187-192.

Prigogine, I. (1997). *The End of Certainty*, ISBN 0684837056.

Prigogine, I. (1993). *Le leggi del caos*, ISBN 88-420-4116-5.

Prigogine, I. (1979). *Vom Sein zum Werden*, ISBN 3-492-02488-2.

Reisenberger, M. P. and Rovelli, C. (2000a). "Spin Foams as Feynman Diagrams." www.arXiv.org/pdf/gr-qc/0002083 .

Reisenberger, M. P. and Rovelli, C. (2000b). "Spacetime as a Feynman Diagram: the Connection Formulation," www.arXiv.org/pdf/gr-qc/0002095.

Ryerson, M. (s. d.). "Design Science and its Goals," http://deed.megan.ryerson.ca/DesignScience.

Sambasivam, S. and Bodas, V. D. (2006). *Entropy. Form Follows Function. Issues in Informing science and Information Technology 3*, ISSN 1547-5840 1, pp. 581-600.

Sartre, J.-P. (1984). *Tagebuecher 1939-1940*, ISBN 3499132923.

Sartre, J.-P. (1943). *L'Etre et le néant*, ISBN 2-07-029388-2.

Sommerfeld, A. (1977). *Vorlesungen ueber theoretische Physik*, ISBN 3-87144-374-3 0 (see in particular vol. 5, 145sqq.).

Spinoza, B. d. (1999). *Ethik in geometrischer Methode dargestellt*, ISBN 3-7873-0969-1.

Spinoza, B. d. (1994). *Theologisch-Politischer Traktat*, ISBN 3-7873-1191-2.

Stauffer, D. and Aharony, A. (1994). *Introduction to Percolation Theory*, 2nd ed, ISBN 0748402535.

Szabó, G. and Fáth, G. (2006). "Evolutionary games on graphs," www.arXiv.org/pdf/cond-mat/0607344 .

Taine, H. (1880). *Der Verstand*. 2 vols. Bonn.

Terpstra, M. (1994). "What does Spinoza mean by 'potentia multitudines'?," in: E. Balibar, H. Seidel, M. Walther (eds.), *Freiheit und Notwendigkeit*, ISBN 3-88479-951-7, pp. 85-98.

Thom, R. (1983). *Mathematical Models of Morphogenesis*, ISBN 0-85312-243-1.

Thom, R. (1975). *Structural Stability and Morphogenesis*, ISBN 0-8053-9276-9.

Thorhauer, Y. (2008). "Ethics of Space Design Based on Lefebvre and Sartre," in: R. E. Zimmermann (ed.), *Perspektivisches Weltverhaeltnis und Raumhaftigkeit der Denkform, (Muenchener Schriften zur Design Science vol. 2)* [in press].

Tosel, A. (1994). *Du Matérialisme de Spinoza*. ISBN 2-908212-77-3.

Van de Vijver, G., Salthe, S. N. and Delpos, M. (eds.) (1998). *Evolutionary Systems. Biological and Epistemological Perspectives on Selection and Self-Organization*, ISBN 0-7923-5260-2.

van Zandt, J. D. (1986). "Res extensa and Space-Time Continuum," in: M. Grene, D. Nails (eds.), *Spinoza and the Sciences*, ISBN 90-277-1976-4, pp. 249-266.

Vickers, S. (2004). *Locales and toposes as spaces*, (Preprint, U Birmingham).

Vollmer, G. (1975/1998). *Evolutionaere Erkenntnistheorie*, ISBN 3-7776-0275-2.

White, D. R. and Harary, F. (2001). "The Cohesiveness of Blocks in Social Networks: Node Connectivity and Conditional Density," [Preprint (Sociological Methodology)], http://citeseerx.ist.psu.edu/viewdoc/summary?doi=10.1.1.16.7875 .

White, D. R., Houseman, M. (2002). "The Navigability of Strong Ties: Small Worlds, Tie Strength and Network Topology," Preprint (Complexity: Special Issue on Networks and Complexity) and SFI research paper, http://repositories.cdlib.org/hcs/DRW2002A/.

Wilson, M. D. (1996). "Spinoza's theory of knowledge," in: D. Garrett (ed.), *The Cambridge Companion to Spinoza*, ISBN 9780521398657, pp. 89-141.

Winkler, B. (1998). *Stadtraum und Mobilitaet. Die Wiedergeburt des oeffentlichen Raumes in Italiens historischen Staedten*, ISBN 3-929638-15-0.

Wolfram, S. (2002). *A New Kind of Science*, ISBN 1-57955-008-8.

Yovel, Y. (1994/1989). *Spinoza. Die Abenteuer der Immanenz*, ISBN 3-88243-296-9.

Yuan, X., Li, H. and Lee, E. S. (2002). *Categories of fuzzy sets and weak topos. Fuzzy Sets and Systems 127*, ISSN 0165-0114, pp. 291-297.

Zimmermann, R. E. (2009). *Topos der Materie. Neue Anleitung zum Glasperlenspiel*, [in preparation].

Zimmermann, R. E. (2008a). "Konzeptuelle Dialektik," (Conference of the Ernst Bloch association on Polyphonic Dialectics, Berlin, 2007), in: Doris Zeilinger (ed.), VorSchein, Nuernberg, in press.

Zimmermann, R. E. (2008b). "Conceptualizing the Emergence of Entropy," *Quantum Biosystems 2*, ISSN 1970-223X, pp. 152-164.

Zimmermann, R. E. (2008c). *Urbane Logik und Topologie der Kommunikation. Über die Hypothesen, welche der Erzeugung von Heimat zu Grunde liegen* [in preparation].

Zimmermann, R. E. (ed.) (2008d) *Perspektivisches Weltverhaeltnis und Raumhaftigkeit der Denkform*, (Muenchener Schriften zur Design Science vol. 2) [in press].

Zimmermann, R. E. (2007a). "Topological Aspects of Biosemiotics," *tripleC 5(2)*, ISSN 1726-670X pp. 49-63.

Zimmermann, R. E. (2007b). *Was heißt und zu welchem Ende studiert man Design Science?* (Muenchener Schriften zur Design Science vol. 1), ISBN 978-3-8322-6413-0.

Zimmermann, R. E. (2007c). "Selbsttranszendenz als Kern evolutionaerer Ethik, EWE," *Deliberation, Knowledge, Ethics, Paderborn, 18/3*, ISSN 1610-3696, pp. 476-478.

Zimmermann, R. E. (2007d). "On the Modality of the World. Space and Time in Spinoza," in: F. Linhard, P. Eisenhardt, (eds.), *Notions of Space and Time, Zeitspruenge 11 (1/2)*, ISSN 1431-7451, pp. 217-244.

Zimmermann, R. E. (2006). "Bewusstsein und Quantenuniversum. Das Ganze auf einen Blick," in: R. E. Zimmermann (ed.), *Naturallianz*, ISBN 3-8300-2111-9, pp.17-38.

Zimmermann, R. E. (2005a). "The Modeling of Nature as a Glass Bead Game," in: E. Martikainen (ed.), *Conference Human Approaches to the Universe. An Interdisciplinary Perspective*. Agricola Society, ISBN 951-9047-94-8, pp. 43-65.

Zimmermann, R. E. (2005b). "River of Blue Fire or the Epistemology of Artificial Worlds," in: R. E. Zimmermann, V. Budanov (eds.): *Towards Otherland. Languages of Science and Languages Beyond* (INTAS Volume 3), ISBN 3899581075, pp. 29-44.

Zimmermann, R. E. (2004a). Graphismus & Repraesentation. Zu einer poetischen Logik von Raum und Zeit. Magenta, München.

Zimmermann, R. E. (2004b). *System des transzendentalen Materialismus*, ISBN 3-89785-422-8.

Zimmermann, R. E. (2004c). "Signaturen. NaturZeichen & DenkZettel. Zur morphischen Sprache welthafter Aktualitaet," *System & Struktur X 1*, ISSN 0944-4475, pp. 18-66.

Zimmermann, R. E. (2002a). *Kritik der interkulturellen Vernunft*, ISBN 978-3-89785-291-4.

Zimmermann, R. E. (2002b). "Diskurse des Unsagbaren. Vorlesungen ueber Hermeneutik," in H. H. Hoier, M. Keller (eds.) *Kleine Schriftenreihe zur Expressionsgeschichte*, Magenta, Muenchen.

Zimmermann, R. E. (2001a). "Beyond the Physics of Logic. Aspects of Transcendental Materialism or URAM in a Modern View," in: *URAM 11* (Ultimate Reality and Meaning. This is also in (2002): *Science & Society* (Polish Academy of Sciences, Scientific Centre, Paris), pp. 17-32. http://www.arXiv.org/pdf/physics/0105094

Zimmermann, R. E. (2001b). "René Thom – Semiologie des Chaos," in: G. Abel (ed.), *Franzoesische Nachkriegsphilosophie – Autoren und Positionen*, ISBN 3-87061-811-6, pp. 185-203.

Zimmermann, R. E. (2000). "Loops and Knots as Topoi of Substance. Spinoza Revisited," http://www.arXiv.org/pdf/gr-qc/0004077v2. The short version is (2002): Spinoza in Context: A Holistic Approach in Modern Terms, in: E. Martikainen (ed.), *Infinity, Causality, and Determinism, Cosmological Enterprises and their Preconditions, Finish Academy of Sciences Colloquium*, ISBN 3-631-39146-3, pp. 165-186.

Zimmermann, R. E. (1999). "Topoi of Emergence," in: K. Bowden (ed.), *ANPA 19, Cambridge (UK), Aspects I*, ISBN 0-9526215-3-3, pp. 86-101.

Zimmermann, R. E. (1998). "Topoi of Emergence. On the Metaphorization of Geometry. Tucson III: Toward a Science of Consciousness. (section 04.03, abstract no. 942)," www.zynet.co.uk/imprint/Tucson/1.htm .

Zimmermann, R. E. (1997a). "Freiheit als Substanz. Metaphysische Aspekte von Initialemergenz und kosmischer Evolution," in: W. Saltzer, P. L. Eisenhardt, D. Kurth, R. E. Zimmermann (eds.), *Die Erfindung des Universums? Neue Ueberlegungen zur philosophischen Kosmologie*, ISBN 3-458-33633-8, pp. 45-71.

Zimmermann, R. E. (1997b). Vom Sein zum Werden oder Auf der Suche nach dem Goldenen Vlies. In: J. R. Bloch (ed.), Perspektiven der Philosophie Ernst Blochs, ISBN 3518582526, pp. 374-390.

Zimmermann, R. E. (1991a). "The Anthropic Cosmological Principle: Philosophical Implications of Self-Reference," in: J. L. Casti, A. Karlquist (eds.), *Beyond Belief: Randomness, Prediction, and Explanation in Science* (Abisko Summer Workshop), ISBN 0849342910, pp. 14-54.

Zimmermann, R. E. (1991b). *Selbstreferenz und poetische Praxis. Zur Grundlegung einer axiomatischen Systemdialektik*, ISBN 3926848162.

Zimmermann, R. E. (1989). "Neue Fragen zur Methode. Das juengste Systemprogramm des dialektischen Materialismus," in: R. E. Zimmermann (ed.), *Jean-Paul Sartre*, ISBN 3-926848-07-3, pp. 44-57.

Zimmermann, R. E. (1988). "Ordnung und Unordnung. Zum neueren Determinismusstreit zwischen Thom und Prigogine," *Lendemains 50*, ISSN 0170-3803, pp. 60-74.

Zimmermann, R. E., Soci, A. and Colacchio, G. (2001). "Reconstructing Bologna. The City as an Emergent Computational System. An Interdisciplinary Study in the Complexity of Urban Structures. Part I: Basic Idea & Fundamental Concepts," www.arXiv.org/pdf/nlin.AO/0109025

Zimmermann, R. E. and Budanov, V. (eds.)(2005). *Towards Otherland. Languages of Science and Languages Beyond*, ISBN 978-3-89958-107-2.

Zizzi, P. A. (2006). "Consciousness and Logic in a Quantum Computing Universe," (ch. 14) in: J. A. Tuszynski (ed.), *The Emerging Physics of Consciousness*, ISBN 978-3-540-36723-9, pp. 457-481.

Zizzi, P. A. (2003). "Spacetime at the Planck Scale: The Quantum Computer View," www.arXiv.org/pdf/gr-qc/0304032 .

Zizzi, P. A. (2000). "Holography, Quantum Geometry, and Quantum Information Theory," *Entropy 2 (1)*, ISSN 1099-4300, pp. 39-69.

www.ingramcontent.com/pod-product-compliance
Lightning Source LLC
Chambersburg PA
CBHW080616270326
41928CB00016B/3079